TWENTIETH CENTURY INTERPRETATIONS

OF

THE TEMPEST

TWENTIETH CENTURY INTERPRETATIONS
OF

THE TEMPEST

A Collection of Critical Essays

Edited by

HALLETT SMITH

Prentice-Hall, Inc.   A SPECTRUM BOOK   *Englewood Cliffs, N. J.*

Current printing (last number):
10   9   8   7   6   5   4   3   2   1

Prentice-Hall International, Inc. (*London*)

For James Thorpe

SMITH, Hallett, ed. Twentieth Century Interpretations of The Tempest; a Collection of Critical Essays. Prentice-Hall, 1969. 114p bibl (Twentieth Century Interpretations) 69-15339. 3.95

CHOICE   OCT. '69

Language & Literature

English & American

An excellent group of essays, all, except for the editor's introduction, published before. One admires Smith's choice of essays which show various attitudes towards *The Tempest*, and one admires most of the essays themselves, even though some were originally passages in books rather than discrete articles. But the librarian must decide on the value of the "Twentieth Century Interpretations" format. Surely almost all of the essays are available in their original form in even small libraries; should the library provide duplicates in a preselected format, even though the selection is a good one? Or is it the place of the library to provide the student with as wide a choice as possible and leave the reprint anthologies to the bookstore?

Contents

Contents

Our revels now are ended. These our actors,
As I foretold you, were all spirits and
Are melted into air, into thin air;
And, like the baseless fabric of this vision,
The cloud-capped towers, the gorgeous palaces,
The solemn temples, the great globe itself,
Yea, all which it inherit, shall dissolve,
And, like this insubstantial pageant faded,
Leave not a rack behind. We are such stuff
As dreams are made on, and our little life
Is rounded with a sleep.

—Act IV, *scene i*

TWENTIETH CENTURY INTERPRETATIONS
OF

THE TEMPEST

Introduction:
The Tempest as a Kaleidoscope

by Hallett Smith

Shakespeare's *Tempest* is a play which has delighted many audiences and many readers. As Hazlitt said, it "is one of the most original and perfect of Shakespeare's productions, and he has shown in it all the variety of his powers. It is full of grace and grandeur." This may well summarize critical appreciation, from Dryden to the end of the nineteenth century. It is an uninterrupted chorus of rhapsodic praise.

Though there is unanimity about the play's quality, there is the greatest diversity of opinion as to what the play means. Furness' Variorum edition collects samples of the sharply contrasting views, up to almost the year 1900. Here we can find Campbell, in 1838, suggesting that Prospero is Shakespeare himself and his magic is his dramatic art. We can learn from Lowell, in 1870, that Prospero represents Imagination, Ariel is Fancy, and Caliban stands for brute Understanding. We can be instructed by Dowden, in 1875, that Ferdinand represents Shakespeare's younger colleague John Fletcher, and the log-carrying is the playwright's discipline. " 'Don't despise drudgery and dry as dust work, young poets,' Shakespeare would seem to say, who had himself so carefully laboured over his English and Roman histories; 'for Miranda's sake such drudgery may well seem light.' " (Miranda represents Art.)

Twentieth-century critics differ among themselves as widely as their predecessors. Some of them are as capable of leading their readers astray as Ariel was of guiding the shipwrecked Italians where he pleased. To keep from wandering too far, it is prudent to bear in mind the date, sources, and structure of the play, its relationship to the other late plays as a group and to relevant earlier plays of Shakespeare's, as well as to the court masque and to the private theater and to music.

The Tempest can be dated with some precision, since there is a record of a performance of it at court on November 1, 1611, and since it borrows some details from accounts of the travels and adventures of Sir George Somers in Bermuda which were not available in England before the fall of 1610. It is, accordingly, a work of 1611, and the last play Shakespeare wrote except for his collaborative labors in *Henry VIII* and *The Two Noble Kinsmen*. It is the culmination of a series of dramatic romances which begins with *Pericles* and includes *Cymbeline* and *The Winter's Tale*.

Shakespeare's plays, written before this series of dramatic romances, are usually divided, as they were in the Folio, into comedies, histories and tragedies. In his earliest efforts as a playwright, about twenty years before the writing of *The Tempest*, he had tried all three kinds—comedy on the Latin model in *The Comedy of Errors*, tragedy of blood and gore in *Titus Andronicus*, and English chronicle history plays in the cycle covering *Henry VI* and *Richard III*. In the following two decades he had perfected each type—comedy in the happy, romantic love-dramas *As You Like It, Much Ado About Nothing* and *Twelfth Night*, history in the stirring *Henry IV* plays and *Henry V*, and tragedy in the sublime magnificences of *Hamlet, Macbeth, Othello* and *King Lear*. For twenty years he had composed, for his company, a play every seven months, on the average. He was a shareholder in the company as well as its principal playwright, and he had prospered. He had bought the second largest house in his home town, Stratford, and he had invested money in land there and in the local tithes. His company had two theaters, the Globe and the Blackfriars, and it also frequently presented plays at court. Life was busy and his fortunes were flourishing, but Shakespeare's interests were turning more and more homeward, to Stratford, and by May, 1612, he had moved there from London. He had a wife there, an unmarried daughter and a married daughter, the wife of a physician, and a four-year-old granddaughter. He was 48 years old.

Probably because *The Tempest* was unpublished and popular, the editors of the First Folio edition in 1623 placed it at the beginning of that volume. Accordingly, the Folio is our only authority for the text. The stage directions, especially for scenes of spectacle, are very full. The copy for the Folio text is thought to have been a transcript by Ralph Crane which reflects with general accuracy the manuscript of the author.

The Tempest is the second shortest play in the whole canon, and it has the fewest scenes. Theatrically, however, it is one of the most spectacular, with an inserted masque, a "quaint device" of a disappearing banquet, a pack of spirits in the shape of hounds, and the storm at sea which opens the play and gives it its name. There is no good reason to suppose the play has been abridged; it is appropriate entertainment for a wedding celebration at court, and it was so given as a part of the festivities for the marriage of the Princess Elizabeth to the Elector Palatine in the winter of 1612–13.

Aside from the travel literature which provided details for the storm and some for the enchanted island, the only positive source for *The Tempest* is a passage in Montaigne's essay "Of the Caniballes" in Florio's translation of 1603. This provides material for Gonzalo's description of an ideal commonwealth in II. i. 147 ff. Caliban's name is an anagram of "cannibal," but the name originally meant merely an inhabitant of the Caribbean, not necessarily an eater of human flesh. For the plot of the play Shakespeare seems to have relied on no particular source, as he did in *Pericles, Cymbeline,* and *The Winter's Tale,* but to have combined motifs which were standard and popular in pastoral romance and in Italian comedy. He had already used a storm in *Pericles;* current interest in Somers's shipwreck in Bermuda made such a scene topical, and Shakespeare was careful to introduce some realistic touches. The popular tale of an exile from court living in some remote place with a royal child or children had of course been exploited in the Bellarius scenes of *Cymbeline;* sometimes this exile was a magician, as he is in the old popular play *The Rare Triumphs of Love and Fortune* (1589). For a duke who, freed of administrative responsibility, yet presides over events like a kind of god, Shakespeare had a model in his own *Measure for Measure.* He had dealt with fairies and spirits in *A Midsummer Night's Dream;* Puck and Ariel perform similar functions, but the differences between the two plays are even more interesting than the similarities. Furthermore, there is actually not very much plot in *The Tempest,* in comparison with the other romances. There are situations, spectacle, music, contrasts of character, and rich poetry in the play which make us overlook the fact that there is no significant dramatic struggle and that actually very little happens. Shakespeare, though he seems to have been readier to borrow plots than to invent them, could without difficulty invent this much.

The most remarkable element of the structure of *The Tempest* is that the play, unlike such romances as *Pericles* and *The Winter's Tale,* obeys the neoclassical unities of place and time. Some critics have supposed that Shakespeare, usually indifferent to the doctrines held by Sir Philip Sidney and Ben Jonson that the action of a play should not cover more than twelve or at most twenty-four hours of imagined time, determined to show his critics that he, too, could write under those rules and turned out a play that covers less than an afternoon. But it is equally possible that he remained indifferent, and that the unity followed naturally from the setting on an island. In *Othello* he had written a play which, after the first act, is confined to an island,

and the last four acts of that play obey the unities with reasonable,
if implausible, fidelity.

Whatever the reason for *The Tempest*'s following the unities, the
effect remains indisputable. There is a concentration and focus in
The Tempest which is found in none of the other late plays and in
few of the early ones. This is related, as Ernest Gohn has pointed out,
to the great emphasis put upon the sense of the present moment in
the play. Prospero's magic depends, of course, upon precise timing;
he says

> I find my zenith doth depend upon
> A most auspicious star, whose influence
> If now I court not, but omit, my fortunes
> Will ever after droop.

He emphasizes "the present business"; he keeps reminding himself
and others that it is "at this hour" or even at this moment, that something must be done. Ariel is incredibly swift in his errands, as he
must be to serve such an exacting and time-conscious master. "Our
revels *now* are ended," Prospero proclaims, and he abjures his rough
magic with the formula "when I have required

> Some heavenly music—which even *now* I do."

The concordance shows that there are more than twice as many uses
of the word "now" in *The Tempest*, a short play, as in any other play
in the canon; the nearest rival is *Hamlet*, a long play. In *The Tempest* truly "the past is prologue" and the present is what matters.
Structure, action, and language combine to reinforce the effect.

Prospero dominates the action of the play. He has created the
storm and he subdues it. He foresees the actions of the other characters
and controls them. The long exposition in I. ii must come from him
because no one else knows the facts; Shakespeare seems comically
aware that such uninterrupted discourse on the stage tends to be
soporific, and Miranda succumbs to sleep. But there are three move-
ments of resistance to Prospero's power and will in the play, and each
one is brought to a climax by a scene of spectacle. Ferdinand and
Miranda resist what they suppose to be Prospero's will in their complete love for each other, and are rewarded, after their ordeal of wood-
carrying, by the masque in IV. i, with the nuptial blessing of Ceres and
Juno and the betrothal dance. The plot of Antonio and Sebastian
against Alonso, King of Naples, is an extension of the original plot
against Prospero; it leads up to the scene of the strange shapes, the
harpy, and the vanishing banquet (III. iii). The conspiracy of Caliban,
Stephano, and Trinculo against Prospero culminates in the theft of

the gaudy garments and the pursuit of the drunken trio by a pack of spirit-hounds (IV. i). Finally, since Prospero controls events and this is a romantic story, all the threads are gathered together when he forgives the offenders, abjures his magic, resumes his dukedom, and prepares to celebrate his daughter's marriage.

Prospero's magic is white magic, not black. He summons up no evil spirits, makes no compact with the devil, and does not jeopardize his soul. The forces he commands are those of nature; he would be regarded by a Jacobean audience in much the way a modern audience views a scientist. His equipment—his staff, robe, and so on—were necessary paraphernalia, but his science came from books, as even Caliban recognizes (III. ii. 99–102). His closest analogue among Shakespeare's characters is Cerimon in *Pericles*.

Prospero's control of natural forces is exercised largely through his familiar spirit, Ariel. At first sight a figure similar to Puck in *A Midsummer Night's Dream*, he should be distinguished by his delicacy and eagerness: "What shall I do? Say what! What shall I do?" "Was't well done?" "Do you love me, Master?" He is a spirit of air, impatient to be free as the air is. He is not a practical joker like Puck, though he can mislead men by mimicry and by his magic as well as his fire. He would never say "Lord, what fools these mortals be!" but rather says that he would sympathize with the charmed prisoners if he were human.

At the opposite pole is Caliban, son of the devil and a witch. He is physically a kind of monster ("moon-calf") and resembles some fabulous sea-monster like a huge turtle ("fish"). Mentally he is incapable of any but practical education; moral principles are beyond him. He is fit only for drudgery but resents it, and his snarling complaint when first summoned, "There's wood enough within!" is typical. His yearning for freedom is in no way respectable, since if he had it he would use it for devilish purposes. Caliban, like Prospero, would seem less strange to contemporary audiences than we often suppose. He is described in the Folio list of characters as "a salvage and deformed slave." Savages had been brought back from America, and the contemporary English interest in them is evidenced by II. ii. 28–34. Caliban fascinated Ernest Renan and Robert Browning in the nineteenth century, and it was in an attempt to explain how Shakespeare could present such a character when he was not imitating anything in actual life that led Dryden to use the word *create* for the first time in a literary sense.

The young lovers, Ferdinand and Miranda, are characterized very economically. Miranda's modesty and innocence are appropriate to the romantic situation in which she is placed—that of never having

seen a young man before. Emerging from a garden of Eden, she wel-
comes the real world of which her elders have grown tired:

> How many goodly creatures are there here!
> How beauteous mankind is! O brave new world
> That has such people in't!

Ferdinand, a pampered prince, gladly undergoes servitude and labor
for his love; he would scorn the baseness of enforced manual work
but for Miranda, whose presence turns it into pleasure and delight.
Ferdinand's willing servitude stands in contrast to the rebellious attitude of Caliban, whose first speech in the play is a refusal to carry
wood.

The cynicism of the villains Antonio and Sebastian is contrasted not
only with the idealism of the young lovers but with the naive, good-
hearted outlook of the "honest old councillor," Gonzalo. The discussion of an ideal commonwealth has repercussions elsewhere in the
play. The idea that man is naturally good seems sufficiently refuted
in Caliban, but the question of the degree of severity with which the
ruling power controls and punishes human wickedness is one in which
the mighty Prospero is still a learner.

The "uninhabited island," as the Folio calls it, which is the scene
of *The Tempest*, is apparently somewhere in the Mediterranean,
since the shipwrecked characters in the play were en route from Tunis
to Italy. Yet the imagery of the play and some of the descriptive detail
concerning the island strongly suggest the New World across the
Atlantic. Shakespeare had read not only the recent pamphlets on the
Somers voyage, but earlier accounts of travel in the western hemisphere
from which he got the name Setebos, a Patagonian devil, and the
knowledge that the Indians in Virginia built dams to catch fish.

The landscape of *The Tempest* is strange and romantic, hardly as
credible as the travellers' tales which Elizabethan readers sometimes
believed and sometimes recognized as lies. In Strachey's *True Reper-
tory* Bermuda is an island with no rivers or running springs of fresh
water, but with an abundance of web-footed shore fowl which were
easy to catch, and very large tortoises or turtles. Prospero's island,
however, has fresh springs, brine pits, barren places and fertile (I. ii.
30). There seem to be no fowl to capture, but one could, if necessary,
survive on "fresh-brook mussels, withered roots and husks wherein the
acorn cradled" (I. ii. 465–67). The native knew where to find berries,
crabs, pig-nuts, and scamels from the rock, whatever they are (II. ii.
172). Caliban says there are bogs, fens, and flats (II. ii. 2) and there
is at least one open place, as in *King Lear*, which affords no shelter
from a storm. It is not easy country to walk through, since it has

toothed briers, sharp furzes, pricking gorse, and thorns (IV. i. 180),
yet in some places the grass grows "lush and lusty," and is green
after a storm (II. i. 51). Gonzalo expected the island to produce whatever necessary for an innocent existence without sweat or endeavor,
but apparently fires are needed and much wood must be carried.
Strangest of all, there is a filthy-mantled pool near Prospero's cell that
is indubitably a horse-pond (IV. i. 182, 200) yet no horses are in
evidence.

The world of *The Tempest* is sometimes the Mediterranean world,
and particularly that of Aeneas's storm-tossed voyage to Carthage and
to Italy. Prospero's great speech on his magic (V. i. 33–35) is based
upon a speech of Medea in Ovid's *Metamorphoses* VII, 197–209.
Shakespeare transmutes his material, whether from current travel
literature or ancient classics, to make his nameless island a place both
credible and strange. Prospero brings in elves from English folklore
as his assistants:

> You demi-puppets that
> By moonshine do the green sour ringlets make
> Whereof the ewe not bites; and you whose pastime
> Is to make midnight mushrumps, that rejoice
> To hear the solemn curfew . . .

Yet his magic, like Medea's, can darken the sun at noon and raise the
dead from their graves.

Reality and illusion constitute a major theme of *The Tempest*.
Many variations are played on it, some comic (as when Caliban and
Trinculo are taken by Stephano as a four-legged monster), some ironic,
as in the deceptions of the villains, and some philosophic, as in Prospero's famous lines after the masque in Act IV:

> Our revels now are ended. These our actors,
> As I foretold you, were all spirits and
> Are melted into air, into thin air;
> And, like the baseless fabric of this vision,
> The cloud-capp'd towers, the gorgeous palaces,
> The solemn temples, the great globe itself,
> Yea, all which it inherit, shall dissolve,
> And, like this insubstantial pageant faded,
> Leave not a rack behind. We are such stuff
> As dreams are made on, and our little life
> Is rounded with a sleep. (IV. i. 148–58)

The incandescent rhetoric of this passage is all the more surprising
in its context, because when he speaks it Prospero is troubled and

distraught. It is, in this way, dramatically inappropriate; it seems obvious that Shakespeare wanted to give this passage special prominence. Its theme, which arises from a comparison of life to the stage, is a familiar one (cf. *Macbeth* V. v. 24–26; *As You Like It* II. vii. 136–66), but here it reaches its ultimate expression.

Of all the plays of Shakespeare, *The Tempest* has the most intimate connection with music. The play has of course a masque-like atmosphere and contains a masque. But it also, short as it is, contains more songs than any other play in the canon. There is also a considerable amount of instrumental music. Much of the music is organic to the plays; indeed, Caliban is witness that "the isle is full of noises, sounds and sweet airs, that give delight and hurt not." Ferdinand is first brought on the stage drawn by one of Ariel's songs; he asserts that the music that crept by him on the waters allayed both their fury and his sorrow. The magical beauty of "Full fathom five thy father lies" would seem to set an almost impossible standard for the lyrics of the rest of the play, but "Where the bee sucks, there suck I" and the rollicking "The master, the swabber, the boatswain, and I" are as superb of their kind. The composer of the songs, and perhaps of the rest of the music for the play, was Robert Johnson, lutenist to the king and supplier of music for many court masques and entertainments.

The verse of *The Tempest* is typical of Shakespeare's final period. It exhibits wide variety, from the stylized rhymed couplets of the masque to the loose rhythms of the dramatic dialogue:

> Full many a lady
> I have ey'd with best regard, and many a time
> Th' harmony of their tongues hath into bondage
> Brought my too diligent ear. For several virtues
> Have I lik'd several women, never any
> With so full soul, but some defect in her
> Did quarrel with the noblest grace she ow'd,
> And put it to the foil. But you, O you,
> So perfect and so peerless, are created
> Of every creature's best! (III. i. 39–48)

It has sometimes caused surprise that Caliban speaks verse though his companions Stephano and Trinculo speak prose. This is not to be taken as indicating that Caliban is more of a poet than they; he is a grotesque but not a comic character, and he is associated with the background of the magic island, which is created largely by poetry.

It is not so easy to find a wealth of imagery in *The Tempest* as it is in the other dramatic romances. This last play is not only thin in plot, by comparison, but also thin in poetic texture. Why this should be so is something of a puzzle. Perhaps the richness of the detail with respect to the exotic island, the dazzling displays of magic, and the pervasive atmosphere of music so engage the imagination that there is little room left for poetic complexity. Or perhaps, as Wilson Knight has suggested, there is less imagery in the verse of this play because the play itself is an image.

The Tempest was apparently appreciated by the Jacobean court, and, according to Dryden, it was played at the Blackfriars, as one would normally expect. On the public stage, after the Restoration, Shakespeare's play gave way to an adaptation by D'Avenant and Dryden, which, with other operatic versions, held sway until the mid-nineteenth century.

For readers it has long been a favorite. Joseph Warton wrote in 1753, "Of all the plays of Shakespeare, *The Tempest* is the most striking instance of his creative power. He has there given the reins to his boundless imagination, and has created the romantic, the wonderful, and the wild, to the most pleasing extravagance." T. M. Parrott in 1949 called it "perhaps the best loved of all Shakespeare's plays."

As to the meaning of *The Tempest*, however, there has been the widest variety of opinion. Because the plot is so simple and the characters so far from complex, the critics find it difficult to account for the great effect the play has upon them. In desperation they turn to biographical, allegorical, religious, philosophical, or psychological interpretations of the play. Apparently the first writer to suggest that *The Tempest* is Shakespeare's personal farewell to his art and his profession was the poet Thomas Campbell in 1838. According to this view, Prospero's abjuration of magic,

> I'll break my staff,
> Bury it certain fathoms in the earth
> And deeper than did ever plummet sound
> I'll drown by book. *Solemn Music* (V. i. 54–57)

is only a poetic way of saying "I'll leave the King's Men, go back to Stratford, and not write any more plays." Some modern writers have considered themselves magicians, but Shakespeare surely did not; everything we know about him contradicts the theory that he would so speak of himself. Other writers apply the allegorical method and see Ariel and Caliban as extensions of Prospero, the former representing an imaginative or spiritual extreme and the latter a physical and material one.

Though E. E. Stoll, in one of the best modern essays on *The Tempest*, gave the warning "that the story is slight is no proof that there is another within or behind it," many critics feel that in this

play more is meant than meets the ear. As one of them (Una Ellis-
Fermor) says, "Shakespeare's utterance in this play is, I believe, like
that of the mystics, definite but comprehensible only to the initiate."
Some critics, professing to be initiate, see the play as an ordeal undergone by Prospero, during which he purifies himself. He is undoubtedly
a rather testy and impatient man, but he finally learns forgiveness
and generosity from Ariel:

> Hast thou, which art but air, a touch, a feeling
> Of their afflictions, and shall not myself,
> One of their kind, that relish all as sharply
> Passion as they, be kindlier mov'd than thou art?
> Though with their high wrongs I am struck to th' quick,
> Yet, with my nobler reason, gainst my fury
> Do I take part. The rarer action is
> In virtue than in vengeance. (V. i. 21–27)

According to this view, the play reaches its dramatic climax when
Prospero forgives his enemies, but a more natural interpretation might
suggest that this is only the preparation for the happy ending of a
comedy.

Those critics who see a very close relationship between *Measure for
Measure* and *The Tempest* will of course find a greater emphasis upon
the theme of justice and mercy than others do. Some (including the
best modern editor, Frank Kermode) see Caliban as more central in
the play than Prospero. Accordingly a major theme is Art and Nature,
as in the other romances. Here there are contrasts: the education of
Miranda with that of Caliban, the love of Ferdinand with the lust of
Caliban, and the white magic of Prospero with the demonic magic
of Sycorax. The doctrine of the play also includes several Platonic
themes, such as the identity of the good and the beautiful and the
importance of chastity. The resonance of all these themes extends
so far for Kermode that he maintains that in *The Tempest* "Shakespeare offers an exposition of the themes of Fall and Redemption by
means of analogous narrative."

A more skeptical view is supported by Stoll and by Northrop Frye,
who maintains that "*The Tempest* is not an allegory or a religious
drama; if it were, Prospero's great 'revels' speech would say, not merely
that all things will vanish, but that an eternal world will take their
place." It is no doubt true that some interpreters of the play empha-
size too heavily small points, such as the statement about prayer in the
epilogue:

And my ending is despair
Unless I be relieved by prayer,
Which pierces so that it assaults
Mercy itself and frees all faults. (Epi. 15–18)

Justice, mercy, forgiveness certainly constitute an important theme in *The Tempest*, but then, so is time a major theme. It may well be that Shakespeare's cast of mind was more Stoic than Christian, and that Prospero's action in forgiving his enemies is to be understood in the light of Seneca's essay on anger rather than as a following of the teachings of Jesus.

The allegorizers and philosophical interpreters run the risk of paying insufficient attention to the charm and delight of the play. That critic will be closest to the truth who responds most fully to its pervasive, enchanting beauty. It is this rather than any arcane philosophical interpretation which has given the play its immortality and caused it to be the progenitor of such vastly different poems as Milton's *Comus*, T. S. Eliot's *The Waste Land*, and W. H. Auden's *The Sea and the Mirror*.

PART ONE

Interpretations

The Tempest

by Sir Arthur Quiller-Couch

The Tempest is the first play in the First Folio of 1623; and this, for aught anybody knows—indeed almost certainly—was its first appearance in print. The Folio, at any rate, supplies our only text. Chronologically it is almost the last, if not the very last, that Shakespeare wrote. The Folio editors, Heminge and Condell, old friends of his and fellow-actors, may have given it pride of place for this pious reason, or possibly because it had won a striking success at Court when presented there in the winter of 1612–13, among many entertainments that graced the betrothal and nuptials of the Princess Elizabeth with the Prince Palatine Elector. John Heminge, as foreman of Shakespeare's old Company, was paid by Lord Harrington, Treasurer of the Chamber of King James I, "upon the councells warrant, dated at Whitehall xxº die Mai, 1613" his bill for producing "foureteene severall playes" in the course of these festivities which were numerous and so costly as to embarrass His Majesty's exchequer. The entry (*Vertue MSS*) specifies these plays, and *The Tempest* comes sixth on the list.

It is pleasant and certainly not impossible to believe that, as Heminge and Condell have preserved it for us, this play was written-up expressly for the betrothal—and presented on Dec. 27, 1612, the betrothal night—of the incomparable Queen of Hearts whose name in story is Elizabeth of Bohemia,

design'd
Th'eclipse and glory of her kind.

For "beauty vanishes, beauty passes," but the charm of this woman still fascinates the imagination almost as in her life-time it won and compelled the souls of men to champion her sorrowful fortunes. That

From "Introduction to The Tempest" by Sir Arthur Quiller-Couch. From The Works of Shakespeare edited by Sir Arthur Quiller-Couch and John Dover Wilson (Cambridge University Press), pp. xlix–lx. Reprinted by permission of Cambridge University Press.

it did this—that it laid on the nobler spirits of her time a spell potent to extravagance and yet so finely apportioned as almost to serve us now for a test and gauge of their nobility—no reader of early seventeenth century biography will deny. The evidence is no less frequent than startling. It would almost seem that no "gentleman" could come within the aura but he knelt to Elizabeth of Bohemia, her sworn knight: that either he followed thenceforth to the last extremity, proud only to serve, or, called away, he departed as one who had looked upon a vision which changed all the values of life, who had beheld a kingdom of the soul in which self and this world were well lost for a dream. We may see this strange conversion in Wotton; we may trace it in the careers of Donne, of Dudley Carleton and (with a postscript of morose disillusion) Lord Herbert of Cherbury. We may read it, youthfully and romantically expressed in this well-authenticated story:

> A company of young men of the Middle Temple met together for supper; and when the wine went round the first man rose, and holding a cup in one hand and a sword in the other, pledged the health of the distressed Princess, the Lady Elizabeth; and having drunk, he kissed the sword, and laying hand upon it, took a solemn oath to live and die in her service. His ardour kindled the whole company. They all rose, and from one to another the cup and sword went round till each had taken the pledge.

We may see this exuberance carried into steady practice by Lord Craven, a Lord Mayor's son, who having poured blood and money in her service, laid his last wealth at her feet to provide her a stately refuge and a home. Through all the story she—grand-daughter of Mary of Scotland, mother of Rupert of the Rhine—rides reckless, feckless, spendthrift, somehow ineffably great; conquering all hearts near her, that

> —Enamour'd do wish so they might
> But enjoy such a sight,
> That they still were to run by her side
> Thoro' swords, thoro' seas, whither she would ride,

lifting all those gallant hearts to ride with her, for a desperate cause, despising low ends, ignoble gain; to ride with her down and nobly over the last lost edge of the world.

We may take it almost for a certainty that—in whatever previous form or forms presented—this play *as we have it* was the play enacted at Court to grace the Princess Elizabeth's betrothal. No argument from internal evidence conflicts with this. Gonzalo's description of his ideal Commonwealth (II. i. 146 *sqq.*) comes out of Florio's translation of

Montaigne, first published in 1603: and the name "Caliban" suggests the essay "Of the Canniballes" from which Gonzalo derived his wisdom. Ben Jonson most likely has a side thrust at *The Tempest* (and at *The Winter's Tale*) in his Introduction to *Bartholomew Fair* (acted in October, 1614): "If there be never a Servant-monster i' the *Fayre*, who can help it, he sayes; nor a nest of *Antiques*? Hee is loth to make nature afraid in his *Playes*, like those that beget *Tales, Tempests,* and such like *Drolleries*." Further, we can easily allow the play to contain many passages suggested by the misadventure of the Virginian voyage of 1609, when a fleet of nine ships and five hundred colonists under command of Sir Thomas Gates and Sir George Somers was dispersed by a gale and the flagship, the *Sea-Adventure,* went ashore on the coast of Bermuda, her crew wonderfully escaping. That Shakespeare used at least one or two out of several pamphlets dealing with this wreck (by Silvester Jourdain, by William Strachey, and by "advise and direction of the Councell of Virginia"—to mention no others) stands above question. But nothing of this is inconsistent either with the play's having been presented by the King's Players on Hallowmas, 1611, or with its having been recast and "revived" for the festivities of the Princess Elizabeth's betrothal.

Nothing forbids our imagination to repeople the Banqueting House and recall this bride, this paragon, to seat her in the front rank of the ghostly audience: to watch her, a moment before the curtain opens, a little reclined, her jewelled wrists, like Cassiopeia's, laid along the arms of her chair; or still to watch her as the play proceeds and she— affianced and, by admission, in love with her bridegroom—leans forward with parted lips to follow the loves of Ferdinand and Miranda.

Those who must always be searching for a "source" of every plot of Shakespeare's (as though he could invent nothing!) will be disappointed in *The Tempest*. Thomas Warton (or rather, Warton misunderstood by Malone) started one false hare by a note in his *History of English Poetry,* vol. III. (1781), that he had been "informed by the late Mr Collins of Chichester"—that is, Collins the poet—that Shakespeare's *Tempest* was formed on a "favourite romance," *Aurelio and Isabella,* printed in 1586 (one volume) in Italian, French and English, and again in 1588 in Italian, Spanish, French and English; the Spanish of Flores being the original. But Collins' mind was darkening towards madness at the time: and *Aurelio,* when found, contained nothing in common with *The Tempest*. Others have followed the clue of a German play, *Die Schöne Sidea,* written by one Jacob Ayrer, a notary of Nuremberg, who died in 1605. There is a magician in this drama who is also a prince—Prince Ludolph: he has a demon or familiar spirit: he has an only daughter too. The son of Ludolph's enemy becomes his prisoner, his sword being held in sheath by the magician's art. Later, the young man is forced to bear logs for Ludolph's daughter. She falls in love with him, and all ends happily. The resemblances to *The Tempest* are obvious: and that there was some actual thread of connexion appears the likelier when we note that "mountain" and "silver," two names of the spirit hounds which Prospero and Ariel set upon the "foul conspiracy" (IV. i. 256), occur in an invocation of Prince Ludolph's in the German play. It may be that Shakespeare used Ayrer's play; for the English Comedians were at Nuremberg in 1604, where they may have seen *Die Schöne Sidea*, to bring home the story. But it is just as likely that Ayrer's is a version of one they took from England to Germany. And, after all, what fairy-tale or folk-tale is commoner, the world over, than that which combines a witch, or wizard, an only daughter, an adventurous prince caught and bound to carry logs, etc., with pity and confederate love to counteract the spell and bring all right in the end?

When we turn to Shakespeare's handling of this story, we first admire that which all must admire, the enchantment wherein he clothes it, the poetic feeling wherewith he suffuses it. Magic and music meet in *The Tempest* and are so wedded that none can put them asunder.

> That was the chirp of Ariel
> You heard, as overhead it flew;
> The farther going, more to dwell
> And wing our green to wed our blue;
> But whether note of joy, or knell,
> Not his own Father-singer knew;
> Nor yet can any mortal tell,
> Save only that it shivers through;
> The breast of us a sounded shell,
> The blood of us a lighted dew.

But when we have paid homage to all this, on second thoughts we may find the firm anatomy beneath the robe—the mere craftsmanship —scarcely less wonderful. For *The Tempest* accepts and masters an extreme technical difficulty. No one can react Shakespeare's later plays in a block without recognising that the subject which constantly engaged his mind towards the close of life was *Reconciliation*, with pardon and atonement for the sins or mistakes of one generation in the young love of the children and in their promise. This is the true theme of *Pericles, Cymbeline, The Winter's Tale, The Tempest*, successively. But the process of reconciliation—especially when effected through

the appeal of sons and daughters—is naturally a slow one, and therefore extremely difficult to translate into drama, which handles "the
two hours' traffic of our stage" and therefore must almost necessarily
rely on the piling of circumstance and character upon one crisis and
its swiftest possible resolution. In attempting to condense such "romantic" stories of reconciliation as he had in his mind, Shakespeare was
in fact taking up the glove thrown down by Sir Philip Sidney in his
pretty mockery of bad playwrights.

> Now of time they are much more liberall. For ordinary it is that two
> young Princes fall in love. After many traverses she is got with child,
> delivered of a faire boy, he is lost, groweth a man, falls in love, and is
> ready to get another child, and all this in two hours' space; which how
> absurd it is in sence, even sence may imagine, and Arte hath taught, and
> all ancient examples justified.

The time supposed to be occupied by the action of *Pericles* is about
sixteen years. *The Winter's Tale* has an interval of about sixteen years
between its third and fourth Acts. The chronology of *Cymbeline* is
baffling and in places absurd; yet it must cover many months. The
once famous Unity of Time is certainly no "law": but it *is* a grace of
drama. And after falling back on such make-shifts as ancient Gower
in *Pericles* and Father Time himself in *The Winter's Tale,* of a sudden in *The Tempest* our artist triumphantly "does the trick." The
whole action of the play, with the whole tale of ancient wrong un-
folded, the whole company of injuring and injured gathered into a
knot, the whole machinery of revenge converted to forgiveness—all
this is managed in about three hours of imagined time, or scarcely
more than the time of its actual representation on the stage.

The *clou* of this feat of stage-craft lies in the famous *protasis* of the
second scene, where Prospero so naturally unfolds all the preliminaries
to his daughter. For exquisite use of *protasis* this may be compared
with the second scene of *Hamlet.* Many critics have praised it: but we
hope that by a few simple stage-directions we have managed to suggest
a beauty which the most of them have missed—the abstracted mind of
Miranda as she listens with a kind of *feyness* to the story so important
on which her father, having chosen and prepared the moment, so
impatiently insists. It is, to our thinking, most necessary to realise
that Miranda is all the while less absorbed by this important story
than by the sea, out of which her fairy prince is surely coming, though
his coming be scarcely surmised as yet. We shall not understand this
play, lacking to understand how young impulse forestalls and takes
charge, outrunning our magician's deliberate contrivance. When Ferdinand and Miranda actually meet

At the first sight
They have changed eyes.

For another point, not over-subtle, which the critics would seem to have overlooked: It is clear to us that the enchantment of the island purposely makes its appearance correspond with the several natures of the shipwrecked men who come ashore. Gonzalo, the "honest old councillor," finds "our garments rather new dyed than stained with salt water." But Antonio and Sebastian cannot see them so. To him "how lush and lusty the grass looks! how green!" Antonio, the total jaundiced villain, sees it "tawny," the half-corrupt Sebastian detects "an eye of green in't"—and so on throughout. Gonzalo indeed is one of Shakespeare's minor triumphs. He is not left—as Antigonus, his counterpart in *The Winter's Tale* was left—to perish after his kind deed. It was done long ago: but he survives, still in his character of loyal-hearted servant, still active in loyalty, which in its turn advances the action of the play. Is it not a delicate stroke that, when Miranda first hears the story of her casting away, of all the shipwrecked company near at hand, though she knows it not, this old councillor is the man she (being heart-whole yet) most desires to see? So in the end he is not only one of the company that awakes Miranda's cry of

O wonder!
How many goodly creatures are there here!
How beauteous mankind is! O brave new world,
That has such people in't!

But for him is reserved the final blessing,

Look down, you gods,
And on this couple drop a blessèd crown!

so unmistakably echoing Hermione's invocation in *The Winter's Tale,*

You gods, look down,
And from your sacred vials pour your graces
Upon my daughter's head!

Caliban has been over-philosophised by the critics (with Renan and Browning to support them). The truth would seem to be that Shakespeare, like a true demiurge, had a tendency to love his creations, and none the less those whom he shows us as gross, carnal, earthy. If it be not unfair to drag Falstaff into the comparison, then even as none of us can help loving Falstaff, so few of us shall we say?—if Caliban came fawning about our legs, would be disinclined to pay him on the head

with a "Good dog! Good monster!" Our sense of justice, too, helps this
instinct: for, after all, Caliban has the right of it when he snarls,

> I must eat my dinner.
> This island's mine, by Sycorax my mother,
> Which thou tak'st from me:

—and we must remind ourselves that in 1611 and thereabouts this dis-
possession of the aborigine was a very present event, however feebly it
might touch the imagination, to trouble the conscience, of our valor-
ous circumnavigators and colonists. Shakespeare, as we conceive him,
differed from Rousseau in most ways, and not least in immunity from
any temptation to construct an ideal portrait of the "noble savage."
But no man can be catholic as Shakespeare was without being fair, and
so (as Hazlitt noted) while the nature of Caliban is the essence of
grossness, there is not a particle of vulgarity in it. Few have remarked
how admirably significant as a set-off to Caliban is Stephano, type of
his predestined conquerors, the tarry, racy, absolute British seaman,
staggering through this isle of magic with a bottle, staring, hiccough-
ing back against Ariel's invisible harp—

> The master, the swabber, the bos'n and I . . .

in extremity to be counted on for the fine confused last word of our
mercantile marine, "Every man shift for all the rest." It is hard to
over-estimate the solidarity of Stephano and the "value" it gives to
the whole fairy picture.[1]

Many critics have lost their hearts to Miranda and no one has ex-
celled Coleridge's praise in delicacy of insight. Let us add but this—
Shakespeare has contrived to mould her of frank goodness and yet
present her as fascinating, captivating by touches so noble that one
can hardly conceive the part adequately rendered save by a princess
in real life as noble as she—an Elizabeth of Bohemia, for example.
She moves to her appointed happiness with fairies and music about
her; but she sees no fairies, sings no song, simply walks straight as the
dictate of her heart directs, and, so walking, steps straight beyond the
magic her father has woven. This incomparable play contains nothing
more subtly simple than her unconscious, quite fearless, outstripping

---

[1] In the list of *dramatis personae* Stephano is merely "a drunken Butler," and
plainly he does not belong to the working crew of the ship, all of whom Ariel has
stowed under hatches. But that he was a seaman his opening song and the general
saltiness of his language make pretty plain. He would seem to have been with-
drawn and given a livery (as the custom was) as superintendent of the King's temporary cellar on shipboard.

of all Prospero's premeditated art. He has drawn around the island a magic circle as that which Ferdinand cannot step across. The play, like *A Midsummer-Night's Dream,* plainly celebrates a betrothal and marches to the fruition of marriage joy. There is much music in both: in both the fairies are made abetters. But whereas in *A Midsummer-Night's Dream* the fairies were Warwickshire elves, playing their pranks anarchically, at their own sweet fancy, to befool mortals, the more rarefied spirits of *The Tempest* obey, under threat, a mortal's compulsion. But Miranda is for the world, gently but fearlessly; on the primal instinct that makes homes, builds and populates cities, recreates and rules the race. Some have objected that this play does not develop; that within Prospero's charmed circle, for the space of three hours, all stands still. In truth a great deal happens, and the ease of its happening is a trick of most cunning preparation.

Who is Prospero? Is he perchance Destiny itself; the master-spirit that has brooded invisible and moved in the deep waters of the greater tragedies, and now comes to shore on a lost nest of the main to sun himself; laying by his robe of darkness to play, at his great ease, one last trick before following the way of the old gods? Is he (as Campbell the poet was the first to suggest) Shakespeare himself, in this last of his plays breaking his wand and drowning his book "deeper than did ever plummet sound"? The lights in the banqueting house are out: the Princess Elizabeth is dust: and as for the island conjured out of the sea for a night's entertainment—

> From that day forth the Isle has been
> By wandering sailors never seen.

Ariel has nestled to the bat's back and slid away following summer or else "following darkness like a dream." But still this play abides, after three hundred years, eloquent of Shakespeare's slow sunsetting through dream after dream of reconciliation; forcing tears, not by "pity and terror" but by sheer beauty; with a royal sense of the world, how it passes away, with a catch at the heart surmising hope in what is to come. And still the sense is royal: we feel that we are greater than we know. So in the surge of our emotion, as on the surges rounding Prospero's island, is blown a spray, a mist. Actually it dims our eyes: and as we brush it away, there rides on it a rainbow; and its colours are chastened wisdom, wistful charity; with forgiveness, tender ruth for all men and women growing older, and perennial trust in young love.

Myth and Miracle

by G. Wilson Knight

The artist expresses a direct vision of the significance of life, and for his materials he uses, for purposes of imitation, the shapes, the colours, the people and events of the world in which he finds himself. But in course of the spiritual progress to which he is dedicated it may happen that the implements of outward manifestation in the physical universe become inadequate to the intuition which he is to express. Art is an extraverted expression of the creative imagination which, when introverted, becomes religion. But the mind of man cannot altogether dispense with the machinery of objectivity, and the inwardness of religion must create, or discern, its own objective reality and name it God. Conversely, the artist, in process of growth, may be forced beyond the phenomena of actuality into a world of the spirit which scarcely lends itself to a purely artistic, and therefore objective, imitation. In *Cymbeline* Shakespeare is forced by the increasing inwardness of his intuition to a somewhat crude anthropomorphism in the Vision of Jupiter: and this anthropomorphic theology is inimical to artistic expression. *Cymbeline* contains a personal god called in to right the balance of a drama whose plot, like that of *Pericles* and *The Winter's Tale,* is incompatible with the ordinary forms of life; but this god, true enough to the religious intuition of the author, yet comes near to exploding the work of art in which he occurs. The form of dramatic art is necessarily extraverted and imitative; and Shakespeare has passed beyond interest in imitation. If a last work of pure art is to be created there is only one theme that can be its fit material. A prophetic criticism could, if *The Tempest* had been lost, have nevertheless indicated what must be its essential nature, and might have hazarded its name: for in this work Shakespeare looks inward and, projecting perfectly his own spiritual experience into symbols of objectivity, traces in a compact play the past progress of his own soul. He is

"Myth and Miracle" by G. Wilson Knight. From The Crown of Life (New York, London, Toronto: Oxford University Press, 1947), pp. 17–28. Reprinted by permission of Methuen & Co. Ltd.

now the object of his own search,[1] and no other theme but that of his visionary self is now of power to call forth the riches of his imagination.

Let me recall the outline of the Shakespearian progress. In the problem plays there is mental division: on the one side an exquisite apprehension of the spiritual—beauty, romance, poetry; on the other, the hate-theme—loathing of the impure, aversion from the animal kinship of man, disgust at the decaying body of death. This dualism is resolved in the tragedies: the hate-theme itself is finely sublimated in *Timon* by means of the purification of great passion, human grandeur, and all the panoply of high tragedy. The recurrent poetic symbol of tragedy in Shakespeare is "storm" or "tempest." The third group outsoars the intuition of tragedy and gives us plays whose plots explicate the quality of immortality: the predominating symbols are loss in tempest and revival to the sounds of music. It is about twelve years from the inception of this lonely progress of the soul to the composition of *The Tempest*.

Now on the island of *The Tempest* Prospero is master of his lonely magic. He has been there for twelve years. Two creatures serve him: Ariel, the "airy nothing" of poetry; and the snarling Caliban, half-beast, half-man; the embodiment of the hate-theme. These two creatures are yoked in the employ of Prospero, like Plato's two steeds of the soul, the noble and the hideous, twin potentialities of the human spirit. Caliban has been mastered by Prospero and Ariel. Though he revolts against his master still, the issue is not in doubt, and the tunes of Ariel draw out his very soul in longing and desire, just as the power of poetry shows forth the majesty of Timon, whose passion makes of universal hate a noble and aspiring thing. These three are the most vital and outstanding figures in the play: for Shakespeare had only to look inward to find them. But there are other elements that complete the pattern of this self-revelation.

Prospero's enemies are drawn to the magic island of great poetry by means of a tempest raised by Prospero with the help of Ariel. In Alonso, despairing and self-accusing, bereft of his child, we can see traces of the terrible end of *Lear*; in Antonio and Sebastian, the tempter and the tempted, plotting murder for a crown, we can see more than traces of *Macbeth*. But, driven by the tempest-raising power of tragic and passionate poetry within the magic circle of Prospero and Ariel, these hostile and evil things are powerless: they can only stand spell-stopped. They are enveloped in the wondrous laws of enchantment on the island of song and music. Caliban, who has been mastered

---

[1] I was thinking "Thou art THYSELF the object of thy search," quoted from H. P. Blavatsky by William James in *The Varieties of Religious Experience*.

by it, knows best the language to describe the mystic tunes of Ariel:

> Be not afeard; the isle is full of noises,
> Sounds and sweet airs that give delight and hurt not.
> Sometimes a thousand twangling instruments
> Will hum about mine ears, and sometimes voices,
> That, if I then had wak'd after long sleep,
> Will make me sleep again; and then, in dreaming,
> The clouds methought would open and show riches
> Ready to drop upon me, that, when I wak'd,
> I cried to dream again. (III. ii. 147)

The protagonists of murder and bereavement are exquisitely en-trapped in the magic and music of Prospero and his servant Ariel. So, too, were the evil things of life mastered by the poetry of the great tragedies, and transmuted into the vision of the myths. The spirit of the Final Plays also finds its perfected home in this the last of the series. Here the child-theme is repeated in Miranda, cast adrift with her father on the tempestuous seas; here the lost son of Alonso is re-covered, alive and well, and the very ship that was wrecked is found to be miraculously "tight and yare and bravely rigg'd" as when it "first put out to sea." (V. i. 224). Prospero, like Cerimon over Thaisa, revives, with music, the numbed consciousness of Alonso and his com-panions; and, as they wake, it is as though mortality were waking into eternity. And this thought makes necessary a statement and a distinction as to the dual possible approaches to the significance of *The Tempest.*

First, we can regard it as the poet's expression of a view of human life. With the knowledge of Shakespeare's poetic symbolism in mem-ory, we will think of the wreck as suggesting the tragic destiny of man, and the marvellous survival of the travellers and crew as another and more perfectly poetic and artistic embodiment of the thought ex-pressed through the medium of anthropomorphic theology in *Cym-beline* that there exists a joy and a revival that makes past misery, in Pericles' phraseology, "sport." According to this reading Prospero becomes in a sense the "God" of the *Tempest*-universe, and we shall find compelling suggestion as to the immortality of man in such lines as Ariel's when Prospero asks him if the victims of the wreck are safe:

> Not a hair perish'd
> On their sustaining garments not a blemish,
> But fresher than before. (I. ii. 217)

So, too, thinking of sea-storms and wreckages as Shakespeare's symbols of human tragedy, we shall find new significance in Ariel's lines:

> Nothing of him that doth fade,
> But doth suffer a sea-change
> Into something rich and strange. (I. ii. 397)

Especially, if we remember that the soul's desire of love in Shakespeare is consistently imaged as a rich something set far across tempestuous seas, we shall receive especial delight in the song:

> Come unto these yellow sands,
> And then take hands:
> Curtsied when you have, and kiss'd
> The wild waves whist. (I. ii. 375)

Commentators divide into two camps and argue long as to the syntax and sense of those last two lines: is "whist," or is it not, they say, a nominative absolute? And if not, how can waves be kiss'd? A knowledge of Shakespeare's imagery, however, is needed to see the triumphant mysticism of the dream of love's perfected fruition in eternity stilling the tumultuous waves of time. This is one instance of many where the imaginative interpretation of a poet, and a knowledge of his particular symbolism, short-circuits the travails and tribulations of the grammarian or the commentator who in search for facts neglects the primary facts of all poetry—its suggestion, its colour, its richness of mental association, its appeal, not to the intellect, but the imagination.

The second approach is this, which I have already indicated. *The Tempest* is a record, crystallized with consummate art into a short play, of all the themes I have discussed in this paper, of the spiritual progress from 1599 or 1600 to the year 1611, or whenever, exactly, *The Tempest* was written. According to this reading Prospero is not God, but Shakespeare—or rather the controlling judgement of Shakespeare, since Ariel and Caliban are also representations of dual minor potentialities of his soul. From this approach three incidents in the play reveal unique interest. First, the dialogue between Prospero and Ariel in I. ii. where Ariel is tired and cries for the promised freedom, and is told that there is one last work to be done—which is in exact agreement with my reading of the faltering art of *Cymbeline*:[2] second, Prospero's well-known farewell to his art, where commentators have seldom failed to admit what Professor Saintsbury calls a "designed personal allegory," and where I would notice that Prospero clearly regards his art as pre-eminently a tempest-raising magic, and next refers to the opening of graves at his command, thereby illustrating again the sequence from tragedy to myth which I have described; and third,

[2] A strange error: whatever our personal likes and dislikes, there is nothing "faltering" in *Cymbeline*.

Prospero's other dialogue with Ariel in **V. i.** where Ariel pities the enemies of his master and draws from Prospero the words:

> Hast thou, which art but air, a touch, a feeling
> Of their afflictions, and shall not myself,
> One of their kind, that relish all as sharply,
> Passion as they, be kindlier moved than thou art? (V. i. 21)

In poetic creation "all is forgiven, and it would be strange not to forgive"; but the partial and fleeting flame of the poet's intuition may light at last the total consciousness with the brilliance of a cosmic apprehension. This speech suggests the transit from the intermittent love of poetic composition to the perduring love of the mystic.

Now these two methods of approach considered separately and in sequence are not so significant as they become when we realize that they are simultaneously possible and, indeed, necessary. Together they are complementary to *The Tempest*'s unique reality. For it will next be seen that these two aspects when considered together give us a peculiar knowledge of this act of the poet's soul in the round: so that the usual flat view of it which reads it as an impersonal fairy story—corresponding to my reading of it as an objective vision of life—becomes a three-dimensional understanding when we remember the implicit personal allegory. Only by submitting our faculties to both methods can we properly understand the play to the full. *The Tempest* is at the same time a record of Shakespeare's spiritual progress and a statement of the vision to which that progress has brought him. It is apparent as a dynamic and living act of the soul, containing within itself the record of its birth: it is continually re-writing itself before our eyes. Shakespeare has in this play so become master of the whole of his own mystic universe that that universe, at last perfectly projected in one short play into the forms and shapes of objective human existence, shows us, in the wreck of *The Tempest,* a complete view of that existence, no longer as it normally appears to man, but as it takes reflected pattern in the still depths of the timeless soul of poetry. And, since it reveals its vision not as a statement of absolute truth independently of the author, but related inwardly to the succession of experiences that condition and nurture its own reality, it becomes, in a unique sense beyond other works of art, an absolute. There is thus now no barrier between the inward and the outward, expression and imitation. God, it has been said, is the mode in which the subject-object distinction is transcended. Art aspires to the perfected fusion of expression with imitation. *The Tempest* is thus at the same time the most perfect work of art and the most crystal act of mystic vision in our literature.

The Tempest

by E. E. Stoll

> Which of you did I enable
> Once to slip inside my breast?
> BROWNING, *At the Mermaid*

There is always a particular interest attaching to the last work of a great author; and in an especial degree this has been true of Shakespeare. If *The Tempest* was not his last play, it would seem that it ought to have been. The action now and then lags a bit, and gives the people on the stage or in the audience a chance to ponder; which the chief character once does to such effect that his speech, of purest and highest poetry, might serve for the "conclusion of the whole matter," *der Weisheit letzter Schluss.* And there are meetings and leave-takings, and glances into the past and at what is to come.

Yet, as I have several times elsewhere indicated, I cannot believe that there is any allegory (which, as in Spenser's *House of Pride,* says one thing and means another), or symbolism (which, as in Tennyson's *Ulysses,* means the thing it says and suggests another), or even "veiled biography" here. *The Tempest,* like every other Shakespearean or popular Elizabethan drama, stands like a tub on its own bottom, is a story in its own right and for its own sake; and unless the intention of the author be of no primary importance, and meanings be not derived from the text but imparted to it, this must be only a rather simpler story of his than usual, a romantic fantasy, precious, not indeed because of the structure or situations, but because of the characters, the poetry, and the rich and dreamy spirit which informs it. That the story is slight is no proof that there is another within or behind it. And Prospero is not Shakespeare any more than (as fewer think) he is James I, except in the sense that the dramatist, not the Scotch monarch, created him; his "potent art" of magic is not the art

From "The Tempest" by Elmer Edgar Stoll. From Shakespeare and Other Masters (*Harvard University Press, 1940*), *pp. 281–83, 299–301, 304–7, 309–13. This material had appeared in an earlier form in PMLA, XLVII (1932), 699–726. Reprinted by permission of the Harvard University Press.*

of poetry; Ariel is not genius, or the lawless imagination, craving liberty but kept in service; Miranda is not the drama; Caliban not the vulgar public; Milan not Stratford; and the enchanted isle not the stage, or London, or the world.

What strange opinions a student of Shakespeare has to contradict! The late Stuart Sherman once said that he was "sorry" for those who do not believe something of the sort; and though thus I am doing only what he was doing, as well as all other people who venture to pity the benighted, I am tempted in turn to be sorry for those—despite their name and number—who believe it. Drama, and character, and poetry do not content them; Shakespeare himself, I fear, does not content them; and with the same noble simplicity "that the author writ" they will not read. They have a medieval or late-Roman taste for an inner meaning, such as that which allegorized Virgil; or the latter-day taste for an inner meaning, which runs into the biographical or symbolical; and particularly in a last work, but in any of moment, they expect to find a "message." Not only do I think such an interpretation unwarranted by the text and the spirit of the poet, I also think it actually troubles and disturbs the artistic effect.

Above all is this true of the characters, especially the mythical ones most eagerly seized upon—Ariel and Caliban. Where does the beauty or greatness of these creations lie if not in their reality? They are not single abstractions personified, but many-sided conceptions incarnated. They are not spirits such as are to be found in Shelley's verse dramas, but beings more actual and convincing than Miranda and Ferdinand themselves. In short, they are not dull, shadowy, or puzzling as the supernatural and allegorical in poetry generally are. Each has his own accent, and personal air, and point of view. Each is interesting in his own right, not by a sort of reversion. And never has the plastic power of the poet asserted itself more emphatically and fruitfully than here, where he had no models in nature to follow. It is as with the fairies in *A Midsummer Night's Dream,* the Weird Sisters and the ghosts in *Macbeth* and *Hamlet.* "Certainly the greatness of this author's genius," says Nicholas Rowe, Shakespeare's earliest editor and himself a competent dramatist, "does nowhere so much appear as where he gives his imagination an entire loose, and raises his fancy to a flight above mankind and the limits of the visible world." For, above mankind (or, in Caliban's case, beneath it), these creations are, though fashioned after its similitude. To be works of art, Shakespeare's ghosts, fates, and sprites, like the angels and demons of Dante and Milton, and the gods and goddesses of Homer and Virgil, are made human, though proportionately. And how by allegory these clear outlines would be troubled, these solid forms dissolved!

Besides, like the ghosts and the Weird Sisters, these two beings are plainly indicated as developments out of popular superstitious conceptions, which are concrete. If Shakespeare meant allegory or symbol he strangely misled his audience, thinking only of the critics to come. In Ariel the tradition is double: he is a sprite like Puck, who gladly serves the king of fairies; and he is the "familiar spirit" of a magician, whom he serves unwillingly. And Caliban is a moon-calf, offspring of a witch and a devil, a conception still current as late as Dryden's day. Unlike and contrasted as they are, they have, as the simple denizens of earth and air, some traits in common: an aversion to labor and a longing for liberty; a primitive sense of humor and a fondness for tricks and pranks; a childish pleasure in tastes and sounds, sights and lights; a spontaneous and unsophisticated love of nature; and (deeper within them) a fear of a higher power, on the one hand, and a craving for affection and approbation, on the other. Thus the contrast between them is heightened.

*   *   *

Six lines are spoken—Ariel, for a contrast,[1] appearing and disappearing, and Prospero repeating his summons—before the mooncalf, cursing, lumbers in. All the malign and baleful operations of nature he can think of he now calls down upon the magician and his daughter, receiving threats in return. Scared by these, he thereupon takes to the defensive and to grumbling.

> I must eat my dinner,

and it is a speech in the same vein as the first. Nothing irritates a servant like being interrupted at that sweet duty, and Caliban stands on his primal rights. Others he remembers forthwith:

> This island's mine, by Sycorax my mother,
> Which thou tak'st from me,

—even as we now unconvincingly say of our Continent, though not born on it, to all newcomers. They, by an illogical but delightfully natural transition, and in the same childish vein, he casts up to his master his kindness in the past and his own gratitude for it.

> When thou cam'st first
> Thou strok'dst me, and made much of me, would'st give me
> Water with berries in't, and teach me how
> To name the bigger light, and how the less,

---

[1] Raysor, *Coleridge's Shakespearean Criticism*, II, 177.

> That burn by day and night; and then I lov'd thee
> And show'd thee all the qualities o' the isle,
> The fresh springs, brine-pits, barren place and fertile.
> Curs'd be I that did so.

And from out of the midst of this appealing whimper he falls, despite his memories, to cursing Prospero anew. He must have release, as the saying now is; for he has not yet developed "inhibitions." "His spirits hear me," he later confesses, "and yet I needs must curse." For only with time do punishments deter.

Never, I suppose, was by thought, word, and rhythm, as well as by mental process, a character so instantly created, and—for I have thus far omitted nothing—so perfectly preserved. Not a false note, anywhere. Caliban is the perfect brute, who would be petted and patted, given food and drink, taught to talk and told stories, yet (with this given as the reason) turns vindictive when he isn't. And what follows is, though startling, as true. When he complains of being "stied in his hard rock," Prospero reminds him that he had lodged him in his own cell until he sought to violate his master's daughter. Then comes the one sexual touch, with the "gros rire ignoble," that Shakespeare permits himself—imagine, with the opportunity, a Joyce or an O'Neill!—

> Oho, Oho! would't had been done!
> Thou didst prevent me: I had peopl'd else
> This isle with Calibans.

No doubt the picture would have been truer with the monster freely wallowing, and art is not morality. It is beauty, however.

* * *

In the next scene where he appears, the monster's tongue, loose enough when last we saw him, is tied, his eyes "almost set in his head." [2] And when he comes to himself he is still full of adulation for Stephano, but of hostility against everybody else. He won't serve Trinculo—he's not valiant. Trinculo calling him a debosh'd fish, he turns to the butler—

> Lo, how he mocks me! Wilt thou let him, my lord?—

and the insult being repeated, he cries,

> Lo, lo again. Bite him to death, I prithee,

[2] A phrase misapprehended by both a German and a French critic. "Deep-set," they say, like a philosopher's, or a zealot's!

for when annoyed not only beasts but children bite. How appealing, like a brute! Resentment is gratitude inverted, is, in the primitive mind, its immediate alternative, and he is still the same creature that had listened wide-eyed to Miranda. Again the insult is repeated, by the mimicry of Ariel; and Caliban bethinks him of punishments more suitable to the offense and occasion, wherein he himself can share:

> Give him blows
> And take his bottle from him. When that's gone
> He shall drink naught but brine, for I'll not show him
> Where the quick freshes are—

so I won't! "I'll bear him no more sticks," he said of Prospero before. And he ha-ha's like a schoolboy at Trinculo's beating, hoping by and by to beat him himself, though now too busy, as he plots against the tyrant. At that thought all his earthy brutality and superstition assert themselves, in appropriate speech. The deed, he would have it done not too delicately, not in the Borgia or Medici style:

> There thou mayst brain him,
> Having first seiz'd his books, or with a log
> Batter his skull, or paunch him with a stake,
> Or cut his wezand with thy knife. Remember
> First to possess his books,

for they are in Latin or gramarye, and it is by the illiterate that writing and print are held most in awe. In return, he will hand over the daughter; for Stephano is master, he but man, and

> she will become thy bed, I warrant,
> And bring thee forth brave brood.

The words smack enough, but not too rankly, of the age of stone.

Ariel, invisible, now troubles them with his mysterious song and tune, and Stephano cries, "Mercy on us." "Art thou afeard?" asks Caliban, pricking up his ears, for the spell of the bottle has lifted. "No, monster, not I." "Be not afeard," he answers, like a child; and then comes the celebrated passage about the isle being full of noises,

> Sounds and sweet airs, that give delight and hurt not,

which has, however, sometimes seemed to me to be a little out of character. Yet an imaginative brute may properly like music as well as stroking and stories; by it Caliban has been made to dream, not as (at our best) we do, but as every now and then a simple soul does next to us at a concert; and then to see the clouds open and show riches ready to drop upon him, that when he waked he cried to dream again. And the like of that still happens in every nursery, high or low.

This child of nature, however, is growing up and, to his cost, learning the folly of his choice. His fellow conspirators won't hold their tongues, and are led astray from their purpose by the plunder—the "trash" or "luggage," as Caliban calls it—at the mouth of the cave. What he foresees befalls them. And when at the end he and the rest are by Ariel ignominiously driven in, he has already fathomed their folly and inanity. Setting eyes now on the gentlemen from the ship, and on Prospero in ducal apparel amongst them, he swears, in an outburst of admiration, but by the god of his mother again, not by him of the bottle:

> O Setebos, these be brave spirits indeed!
> How fine my master is! I am afraid
> He will chastise me.

The strangers are spirits to him, as Columbus and his crew were to the Indians, and as a newcomer in town was thought to be possibly a god in disguise by the Homeric Greeks. Rebellion, moreover, is already in full reaction. Prospero is master again, and the servant by his very nature is servant again, to the point that he takes a delight in his master's finery but, by another psychological transition, bethinks him of what is coming next. The transitions of his thoughts, indeed, the succession of his emotions, are among the happiest touches in the role. He thinks like a savage, without uttering all that a savage thinks. But Prospero sets him to work trimming the cell; and Caliban shows that he has already learned his first lesson in the values and limitations of life as he good-humoredly accepts the order, muttering:

> What a thrice-double ass
> Was I to take this drunkard for a god
> And worship this dull fool!

Nature is justified of her child: he acquires something of what she could not transmit but has bestowed the capacity of acquiring—the faculty of Common Sense. His last unromantic, unexpected speech is the most delectable touch of all. Who in the whole world is like Shakespeare? Why, Chaucer, and Fielding, and Scott, and the English people.

*   *   *

There is much else to be said of *The Tempest*—of Miranda, whose love affair is not exciting, but whose character, though without Perdita's or Imogen's spirit and humor, is not, as some recent critics have declared, insipid; of the relations of the father and daughter, which are exquisite; and of the action as a whole, which, owing to the magician's omnipotence, is, for all the good moments, somewhat meager and dull. By some of the Germans Prospero has been taken psychologically, as having lost the dukedom, not really through a brother's treason but by his own withdrawal from reality, and as having mended his ways (like those, I suppose, who learn to skate in summer and to swim in winter) on a desert isle. By Shakespeare his downfall is explained as wholly owing to the machinations of Antonio; and Prospero's failure then and there to employ against him the magic arts which later are so efficacious is not explained at all. This, like other initial postulates in Shakespeare, and in many another dramatist before and after, must simply be granted: and a psychical defect is no more to be discovered in this deposed duke than in that of *As You Like It,* or in the disguised one of *Measure for Measure,* or in the rejected one of *Twelfth Night.*

Like Rosalind's father, moreover, this duke is glad to return to power; (he and his daughter seem much less interested in their uninhabited island than the other and his followers in the wood of Arden). No one seems to delight in it but Caliban, who was born on it (for Ariel is of the elements, and follows summer like a swallow); and indeed the chief reason that I can see for *Milan's* being Stratford is that from Nature both Duke and daughter seem glad to get away. So for us too the isle is a disappointment, enchanted, but—and here, again, the difference between Elizabethan fact and present-day figure—not enchanting. Only through the limited sensibilities of Caliban do we know it. It is full of noises, but they are Ariel's sweet airs, not the native woodnotes wild. And that it *is* wooded we scarcely should be aware except for Caliban's and Ferdinand's forced labor, Ariel's penitentiary pine, and Stephano's threat to Trinculo of the nearest tree. Shakespeare himself seems uncertain, for in a previous scene Trinculo has crept under the monster's gabardine because "here's neither bush nor shrub"; and in the Masque the scenery and vegetation are of field and pasture, not of the wilderness at all. But a virgin forest, on a virgin island, with rocks and flowers and fountains, under unfamiliar and unclouded constellations, encircled by tropical seas! What would not Coleridge, Shelley, or Keats have made of it, Chateaubriand or Heine! Milton would have given it mystery—if not of novelty, then of reminiscence, and of time and space, of light and shade; even Spenser, who, like everybody with a soul, delighted in islands, would have made it into a romantic, though scarcely a wild, primeval spot. Ordinarily, though Shakespeare had less interest than the latter in discovery and the New World, he had far more in Nature

unsophisticated, in bird, beast, and flower, river and sea; and before
this he had filled the woods of Athens and Arden with life and charm:

> I know a bank where the wild thyme blows . . .

> Under the greenwood tree
> Who loves to lie with me
> And turn his merry note
> Unto the sweet bird's throat . . .

> Under the shade of melancholy boughs
> Lose and neglect the creeping hours of time.

Even the poetry of desolation is missing—"there let the wind sweep
and the plover cry!"—and Prospero and Miranda leave the island to
Caliban, with a farewell only for Ariel and the elves.

And that leads to a further consideration, the pervading spirit of
the play. Since the chronology was established, criticism has delighted
in these last works of the poet's pen, *The Tempest, The Winter's Tale,*
and *Cymbeline,* not only as a farewell to his art but as a revelation of
his personal experience. It has found in them, after the darkness and
despair of the tragedies, a spirit of serenity and reconciliation; and,
in the flowers and pastoral landscape, the gallant youths and pure-
minded maidens, something of Stratford again. Even scholars are
inclined to think that they must have been written there; on the same
principle as that of the tradition that the ghost scene in *Hamlet* must
have been written there, hard by the churchyard and the Charnel-
House.

An optimism, or a delight in Nature, either, that depends upon the
present experience of the poet, would count for little. Moreover, the
supposition, as Mr. Sargeaunt says, "puts a strange construction on an
artist's activity. For is it not the irreconcilability, the irrationality of
actual experience, which sets him to the creation of life in art?" [3] Even
as a man the poet would, more probably, have been thinking of the
pastoral in London, from afar. But in fact, as Mr. Lytton Strachey,[4]
who also rejects the supposition, clearly shows, these last plays, including the one now before us, are not altogether serene. Dowden and
his followers apply to the period of the tragedies the expression "Out
of the Depths"; to that of the dramatic romances, "On the Heights."
But in this final period there is a measure of ugliness and horror,
cynicism and grossness. There are the intended crimes of Iachimo,
Cloten, and Cymbeline's Queen, Antonio and Sebastian, and the

---

[3] *Times Literary Supplement,* December 15, 1932, "The Last Phase."
[4] *Books and Characters* (1922). The quotations in the next paragraphs are at pp.
58, 59, 60, 63 (by permission of Harcourt, Brace & World, Inc.).

murderous jealousy of Posthumus and Leontes. And the maidens Imogen and Miranda show a familiarity with unmaidenly ideas, and Prospero insists upon them, in a way that somewhat grates upon us. Why should he warn Ferdinand, about to be left a moment with Miranda, not to break her virgin-knot, and then, the next moment, harp on the subject again? Why, before that, when, mistaking, she asks him whether he is not her father, should he in reply take to the musty old joke of her mother's word; and then, before the scene is over, as, speaking of Antonio's perfidy, he wonders "if this might be a brother," why should the daughter in turn apply it to her grandmother?

Here is still another instance of the critics' not reading but reading *in;* and, as Mr. Strachey says, "this combination of charming heroines and happy endings [and the flowers, we might add, in *Cymbeline* and *The Winter's Tale*] has blinded the eyes of modern critics to everything else." Of delight in Nature for her own sake there is in these plays less, it would seem, than in the earlier ones. Prospero himself, as the impersonation of Shakespeare, Mr. Strachey finds to be no compliment to the poet, and complains of his crustiness. And there is some truth to this, though Prospero's harshness is mainly owing to the poverty of the plot. No obstacles opposing his omnipotence from without, one must be raised up within. Since Miranda, the ingénue, is ready to fall into Ferdinand's arms like a brook into the river, he must stand between them with his menaces and tasks; and since Ariel and Caliban have otherwise little personal interest in the outcome, he must thwart their longings for liberty or idleness. But Mr. Strachey is right enough in saying that "it has often been wildly asserted that he is a portrait of the author—an embodiment of that spirit of wise benevolence which is supposed to have thrown a halo over Shakespeare's later life." For though the critic goes pretty far in declaring that on closer inspection "both portrait and original are imaginary," Prospero himself, after all allowances, is too often dull or sour.

The Enchanted Island

by John Dover Wilson

Many writers assume that Shakespeare was more or less of a convalescent in his last years, that his grip was loosening and his brain softening. I can see no evidence whatever for this in the plays themselves. Turning to invent a new form of drama to match a new mood, Shakespeare as usual experiments before he achieves exactly what he aims at, and by the side of *The Tempest* its immediate predecessors, it is true, seem loose-knit. Yet they are lovely things in themselves —*Cymbeline,* it must be remembered, was Tennyson's favourite play, and his precious copy was buried with him; while *The Tempest,* as a piece of sheer artistry, is surely the most consummate of all Shakespeare's masterpieces. But why did not Shakespeare write anything after *The Tempest?* Is there not something odd, enquires the Shylock school of criticism, in a man giving up a lucrative profession at the age of forty-eight, leaving London at the height of his fame, and retiring to an obscure provincial town like Stratford? And there follows talk of Bright's disease, or even worse things are whispered.

The problem of the retirement is, as I shall later show, closely related to that of the "conversion." But two things may be said at once about it. In the first place, the break with London in 1612 was clearly deliberate, and a decision taken when Shakespeare was apparently in perfect health. *The Tempest* proves this; for *The Tempest,* as most readers have agreed, is on the face of it Shakespeare's farewell to the theatre, and *The Tempest* was not written by a sick man. And in the second place, there is not a hint either in contemporary record or local tradition that Shakespeare suffered disability or disease of any sort during his later years. On the contrary, all we can glean points to cheerfulness and happiness. His first biographer Rowe, writing in 1709, declares that "the latter part of his life was spent, as all men of good sense will wish theirs may be, in ease, retirement, and the conversation

From "The Enchanted Island" by John Dover Wilson. From The Essential Shakespeare *(Cambridge University Press, 1932), pp. 131–45. Reprinted by permission of the Cambridge University Press.*

of friends," while he also asserts that Shakespeare was well acquainted with many gentlemen of the neighbourhood. There were visitors too from London. We are told of a convivial meeting with Drayton and Ben Jonson shortly before the end, which does not suggest failing health and certainly suggests high spirits. The information comes from John Ward, vicar of Stratford from 1662 to 1681, who adds "it seems" that they "drank too hard, for Shakespeare died of a fever there contracted." The supposition of the parson we may discount, like the tale of dying a papist. But we have no reason to disbelieve his statement about the "fever"; many in Stratford as early as 1662 would remember what the great man died of, and Ward who was interested in medicine would take careful note of such a fact. Shakespeare, we may therefore assume, was carried off by some epidemic four years after he had turned his back upon London.

To understand Shakespeare's retirement, we must return to 1608, try and fathom his "conversion," and study his last plays. For here as in everything else about him the poet was father to the man, and Keats is the truest guide when he tells us that "Shakespeare led a life of allegory; his works are the comments upon it."

As I have said, sickness of body as well as sickness of spirit there may well have been after the completion of *Lear,* but illness is not necessary to explain the lifting of the clouds in *Antony and Cleopatra,* the ebb of the tragic tide visible in *Coriolanus,* the dawn of a new mood in *Pericles* and *Cymbeline.* And the "conversion" itself is of course a poetic one—none the less real or profound for that! Accordingly we must go for helpful analogies, not to the theological or moral sphere, but to the realm of art.

Beethoven's last phase possesses points of similarity which it would be fascinating to explore, had I the musical knowledge or insight. Let me instead briefly consider three literary parallels. First there is *The Book of Job,* that marvellous poem on the meaning of the universe, a theme which it handles artistically and not philosophically, exactly as Shakespeare handles it in *Lear.* But *Job* embraces more than *Lear;* it includes the recovery as well as the anguish. And what is it that brings the recovery about? Certainly not the philosophers; there are three of them, each with his special solution, and they are called "Job's comforters" because they bring no comfort. The healing comes, neither from argument nor statement, but from a contemplation of the beauty of the world, the morning stars singing together, the majesty of the sea, the strength and loveliness of the animals, the glory of the creation of God. Or take Dostoieffsky, whose cosmic novels are the nearest approach to Shakespeare's tragedies in modern literature. He too in the terrible *Crime and Punishment, The Idiot,* and *The Pos-*

sessed treads the razor-edge and only comes through as by a miracle.
In the last and greatest of his books, which has points of affinity with
The Tempest, the miracle is in part explained, and we see that salva-
tion has been won through a return to the grand simplicities of life,
typified by the divine Alyosha and his boys, and by the story of the
marriage at Cana of Galilee.

But Shakespeare was English, and the closest analogy to his conversion is that of another English poet, a poet who experienced it at the
beginning not near the end of his career, who had nevertheless, like
Shakespeare, passed through a spiritual crisis, leading him to the gates
of madness, who had dreamed of an age of reason,

> France standing on the top of golden hours,
> And human nature seeming born again,

had seen the vision dissolve in blood and terror; and had come to
realise that the attempt to overthrow the social structure meant striking at the very roots of the spirit of man. Gradually, by the help of a
woman, his sister (as Shakespeare perhaps by his daughter), the
spiritual convalescent recovered his lost self and his first love, his love
of the countryside on which his infant eyes had rested, amid which
he had grown to manhood, from which he had learned to become a
poet. The revulsion of feeling was complete. He seemed to have
escaped from subjection to some barren witch who had offered him an
impossible and detestable mirage in exchange for the paradise that lay
around him. Nature, the birds, youth, the peasant, the simple traffic
of family life, all that drew blood from that accumulated wisdom of
centuries which we call instinct and tradition, were the only teachers,
the only healers.

I use words I wrote about Wordsworth five years ago, without a
thought of Shakespeare in my mind. The parallel is not exact, of
course; history does not repeat herself. But the crisis and its occasion,
the conversion and its cause, are extraordinarily similar. Wordsworth
recovered by falling in love a second time with the Lake country;
Shakespeare by falling in love a second time with Stratford. But let
Wordsworth himself speak for the creator of *Lear*.

> These beauteous forms,
> Through a long absence, have not been to me
> As is a landscape to a blind man's eye:
> But oft, in lonely rooms, and 'mid the din
> Of towns and cities, I have owed to them,
> In hours of weariness, sensations sweet,
> Felt in the blood, and felt along the heart;

> And passing even into my purer mind,
> With tranquil restoration. . . . Nor less, I trust,
> To them I may have owed another gift,
> Of aspect more sublime; that blessed mood,
> In which the burthen of the mystery,
> In which the heavy and the weary weight
> Of all this unintelligible world,
> Is lightened:—that serene and blessed mood,
> In which the affections gently lead us on,—
> Until, the breath of this corporeal frame
> And even the motion of our human blood
> Almost suspended, we are laid asleep
> In body, and become a living soul:
> While with an eye made quiet by the power
> Of harmony, and the deep power of joy,
> We see into the life of things.

There is no more wonderful description of poetic ecstasy in all poetry than this, and there is no better illustration of its truth than *The Tempest*. Wordsworth explains the last plays of Shakespeare, and the last plays lend to Wordsworth's lines the force of a new revelation.

Shakespeare fell in love with Stratford, with its memories, its quiet pastures and wide skies, with all the wild life of bird and beast and flower, with the pleasant friendships and domesticities of the little town, with his house and garden, with his own family, and especially perhaps with his younger daughter. Can any explanation of his retirement be more natural and more complete than this, if we remember that when poets love they love with a passion which cannot be gainsaid? One can feel it growing in the plays, from the contrast drawn by Bellarius between the slippery life of the court and the honest freedom of the countryside, through the sheep-shearing scene of *The Winter's Tale*, up to the inaccessible island cut off from civilisation, full of

> Sounds and sweet airs that give delight and hurt not.

But most of all is it felt in the innocent figures, especially of young girls, that now take the centre of his stage: Marina, playing with her flowers by the water's brink, Imogen and the "flower-like boys, Guiderius and Arviragus," Perdita as Flora at the country-feast with her Florizel, and to crown all, the peerless couple Miranda and Ferdinand.

It meant of course giving up his art, for though *The Tempest* at any rate was I think mostly written at Stratford, that was not Shakespeare's way and in the nature of things could not last. So a choice had to be made, and *The Tempest* tells us what it cost him.

And yet, he had surely given the world enough! Twenty years'
slavery at his desk, and the handling of thirty-six plays; what more
did they want? If he stayed on in London, could he ever write better
love-plays than *Romeo and Juliet* and *Antony and Cleopatra*, or better
comedies than *As You Like It* and *Twelfth Night*, or better tragedies
than *Othello*, *Lear* and *Macbeth*, or better fairy-plays than *A Midsummer-Night's Dream* and *The Tempest*; or create greater characters
than Shylock, Falstaff, Hamlet, Lady Macbeth, and Cleopatra? His
company could get on without him; dramatists had become plentiful,
and this Beaumont and Fletcher pair had the trick to entertain the
court people well enough. Not that there was any fear of his own plays
going out of fashion; as long as there were King's Men in England
and a King to perform for, they would be in demand—he knew their
worth. Some folk would have him print them; but printing was bad
business for a playhouse, and the printing-press was a new-fangled toy
which had never taken his fancy. Neighbour Field had made a fair
job of those poems of his which had pleased his patron; what he had
seen of printed plays, however, had not pleased him, least of all the
plays of his own which actors had stolen or the company had sold to
publishers in hard times. Besides plays were not books at all; that was
one of Ben Jonson's mistakes. Ben talked of publishing "his works,"
but he was a bookman, even a little of a pedant, and never could
understand that plays were like music which only came alive when
performed. And though retirement to Stratford meant giving up the
stage, one could always write poetry. *Venus and Adonis, Lucrece,* and
the sonnets were juvenile stuff; he had had no time since to attempt
anything more in that sort. But if the fit came upon him, it had to
take its course, and at Stratford. . . . First of all, however, he must
order his house and garden; and he needed rest, intermission from
writing, for a space of years at least.

Four years were granted. Who knows what ten or a dozen might
have brought forth for English literature, or even whether his puritan
son-in-law Dr. Hall may not have quietly suppressed "pagan verses"
found in his study of books after his death?

And so the last plays are the last we have of him. Taken in order
they show "the burthen of the mystery"

> the heavy and the weary weight
> Of all this unintelligible world

growing ever lighter as

> that serene and blessed mood,
> In which the affections gently led him on

became more and more habitual. But, being the most honest poet who ever breathed, he was not going to seek an easy though false security by escape. He clung to the old mood, almost in desperation; there are more fearful scenes in *Pericles,* despite its happy ending, than in *Antony and Cleopatra.* At the outset his method is simply one of contrast, white against black, Marina the dove of innocence in the brothel, or the radiant and spotless Imogen disrobing herself while foul Iachimo lurks in his trunk. But the atmosphere of a drama depends upon its total effect, and especially the effect left by the concluding scenes. Put to the test of theatrical performance, all four plays appear as plays of reconciliation and forgiveness. Shakespeare had always grown tender, right from the beginning, at the thought of pity, mercy, forgiveness; and his worship of them had shown itself sublime in the scenes between Lear and Cordelia. It is therefore natural enough that they should assume special prominence in the romances. Yet one cannot help wondering whether their presence in these plays was not somehow connected with the return to Stratford. Was there some feud to compose, some wrong to make amends for, before the owner of New Place could say "The air breathes upon us here most sweetly"?

In *The Winter's Tale* the two worlds are treated in a fresh and more satisfactory fashion. We begin with a little jealousy play complete in itself, Leontes being an ignoble Othello; the second part is entirely given up to the brave new world of love and beauty and innocence; and then the two are brought together cunningly in the reconciliation scene of the living statue. *The Winter's Tale* is one of the tenderest and loveliest of all Shakespeare's dramas, but it did not content him. Two separate worlds, the blessed world and the bitter world, even when reconciled in a finale do not make either one world or one play. For the problem was both a technical and a spiritual one, as is generally the case with Shakespeare, and indeed with all poets who attempt to span the whole of life. It was a problem, let me insist again, of art, not of morals or philosophy or theology. If he could once attain a vision of the two worlds and his two moods as a single harmonious whole, and could express that vision in a play as perfect in its way as *King Lear,* his spirit would be at rest and he would have earned his Stratford.

And one day the vision came, came as things often did with him from some chance event of the hour. Late in 1610 news reached London of a wreck off the Bermudas in which an English ship had gone aground and those on board had, miraculously as it seemed, come to shore upon an island very fertile but reported by all as enchanted. The news and the excitement it caused gave him his topic, and the topic solved his problem. The play should begin daringly with a wreck and a tempest, so realistic and overwhelming in its effect, that the audience would be ready to suspend all disbelief in the marvels that followed. For on the enchanted island he would bring the wrongers and the wronged together, and the two worlds should be harmonised at one spot and at one point of time. Harmonised, not opposed as on a battle-field—he would so work it that the injurers should "lie all at the mercy" of the injured, and should then be over-come, not through punishment or revenge, but by means of forgive-ness and reconciliation, a reconciliation which should be sealed by love, by the blessed union of innocents from both worlds, too young to have inherited the wrongs or the guilt of either.

Sofar, except for the technical advance of the unity of space, time, and atmosphere, the theme was much the same as that of *Pericles, Cymbeline,* and *The Winter's Tale.* Yet *The Tempest* altogether transcends the aim and scope of its predecessors, and it does so largely because of this unity, or rather through the island, which is the means whereby unity both dramatic and spiritual is secured. For, what is the enchanted island but Life itself, which seems so "desert and unin-habitable" to the cynics and so green with "lush and lusty" grass to the singleminded? It is Life also as Shakespeare himself sees it with his recovered vision; once the domain of a foul witch, but now beneath the sway of a magician who controls it entirely, who keeps the evil spirits in subjection and employs the good spirits to serve his ends, and so has banished fear from it.

> Be not afeard—the isle is full of noises,
> Sounds and sweet airs that give delight and hurt not:
> Sometimes a thousand twangling instruments
> Will hum about mine ears; and sometimes voices,
> That, if I then had waked after long sleep,
> Will make me sleep again—and then in dreaming,
> The clouds methought would open, and show riches
> Ready to drop upon me, that when I waked
> I cried to dream again.

How like that is to Wordsworth in feeling, how unlike in expression!

What then is Prospero who works these marvels? He reminds us of Lear, a wronged old man, but a happier Lear with his Cordelia to share his banishment. There is, too, much of Shakespeare himself in him, as has often been observed; and I have no doubt that the dis-missal of Ariel and the lines:

> I'll break my staff,
> Bury it certain fathoms in the earth,
> And deeper than did ever plummet sound
> I'll drown my book—

are his hinted farewell to the theatre, while the speech which precedes these lines is surely intended to depict the tragic mood he has just escaped. Prospero, again, has learnt that Desire may prove a savage beast, and has chained it up in a rock beneath his cell. Yet he is more than Shakespeare, he is Dramatic Poetry; just as the island is more than Life, it is Life seen in the mirror of ripe dramatic art, Life seen

> not as in the hour
> Of thoughtless youth; but hearing oftentimes
> The still sad music of humanity,
> Not harsh nor grating, though of ample power
> To chasten and subdue.

Prospero is a magician; but all that he performs is wrought by means of Ariel, who is poetic imagination. Even the turning-point of the play, his conversion from the thought of revenge to thoughts of pity and forgiveness, is prompted not by moral or religious considerations, but by Ariel. Thus Shakespeare anticipates Shelley's famous doctrine: "The great instrument of moral good is the imagination; and poetry administers to the effect by acting upon the cause." And the apocalyptic vision of the universe to which he gives utterance at the end of his masque, what is it but an interpretation of Life as a sublime dramatic poem?

> Be cheerful, sir.
> Our revels now are ended: these our actors,
> As I foretold you, were all spirits, and
> Are melted into air, into thin air,
> And like the baseless fabric of this vision,
> The cloud-capped towers, the gorgeous palaces,
> The solemn temples, the great globe itself,
> Yea, all which it inherit, shall dissolve,
> And like this insubstantial pageant faded,
> Leave not a rack behind: we are such stuff
> As dreams are made on; and our little life
> Is rounded with a sleep.

Is *The Tempest* a Christian play? It is surely a profoundly religious poem, and of a Christ-like spirit in its infinite tenderness, its all-

embracing sense of pity, its conclusion of joyful atonement and forgiveness, so general that even Caliban begins to talk of "grace." But it
is not in the least Christian from the theological standpoint; there is
no word of God, not a hint of immortality. On the contrary, rewrite
the passage just quoted in scientific prose, and we find ourselves con-
fronted with an icy universe, utterly regardless of man and destined
to ultimate extinction, which reminds us of the philosophy of Bertrand
Russell. But it is not science either, and instead of depressing it ele-
vates the spirit with the grandeur of the spectacle it presents and the
magnificence of the rhetoric in which it is clothed. Questions of fact
and of opinion are irrelevant here. We are in a realm beyond reason
or belief; we are sharing in the beatific vision of the greatest of all
dramatic poets,

> While with an eye made quiet by the power
> Of harmony, and the deep power of joy,
> We see into the life of things.

The Tempest is not then the subject of argument or explanation; it
is to be accepted and experienced. Even my attempt to catch glimpses
of a personal view behind its divine ecstasy (in order to rebut a power-
ful critic who regards the drama as a kind of hothouse, with an
atmosphere compounded of disgust, boredom, and phantasmagoria)
misleads and offends; for, use it how we will,

> Our meddling intellect
> Misshapes the beauteous forms of things.

If we are to talk about *The Tempest,* it must be as poetry; or to
compare it with anything else, it must be with other dramatic poems.
It is, for instance, at once the completion and the obverse of *King
Lear.* In *King Lear* Shakespeare succeeded in showing Truth, at its
bleakest and most terrifying, as Beauty; in *The Tempest* he succeeded
in showing Beauty, at its serenest, most magical and most blessed, as
Truth. And if we are to seek his faith, we must go not to the creeds
but to the poets. Keats is his nearest of kin, and the confession of Keats
might have been his also:

> "Beauty is truth, truth beauty,"—that is all
> Ye know on earth, and all ye need to know.

Shakespeare's Last Plays

by Theodore Spencer

The Tempest carries the theme a step further, and it is tempting to see in this last of Shakespeare's complete plays both his final treatment of the difference between appearance and reality and his final presentation, transformed by a new imaginative vision, of the three levels in Nature's hierarchy—the sensible, the rational, and the intellectual—which formed the common psychological assumption of his time. If we succumbed to that temptation, we would claim that the play shows a temporary, apparent, evil dispelled by a lasting, real, good, and that Caliban represents the level of sense, the various noblemen the untrustworthy level of reason, and Prospero with his servant Ariel, the level of uncontaminated intellect. *The Tempest* might thus be made the final piece in an ordered pattern of fully developed insight, a dramatization, based on a new interpretation of Nature's distinctions, of a final vision of redemption and the triumph of goodness.

But the play itself, like all of Shakespeare's work, like human life, defies any scheme so neat and so mechanical. The common assumptions are no doubt present, a part of the texture, but the play is very far from being a mere illustration of them. The characters and the action have a more individual value, hence a more universal significance, than could be given them as mere illustrations of a scheme. Nor can we say, as Prospero returns to his kingdom and Miranda is united to Ferdinand, that there is any universal triumph of goodness. Evil beings incorrigibly still exist, though they are no longer in control nor at the center; the center is edged with darkness, though our eyes may be directed at the central light of transfiguration and restoration. In a world of recreated and newly fashioned relationships there is still a silent Antonio who scowls alone.

Yet, though there is nothing mechanical about their presentation,

From "Shakespeare's Last Plays" by Theodore Spencer. From Shakespeare and the Nature of Man *(New York: The Macmillan Company, 1942), pp. 195–99. Copyright © 1942 by The Macmillan Company. Reprinted by permission of the publisher.*

the familiar levels of value do exist in the play, and to be aware of them may help us to understand it. Caliban, complicated character that he is, does primarily represent the animal level; the "beast Caliban," as Prospero calls him, is a thing "not honor'd with human shape" (I. ii. 283); he is set apart—as it were abstracted—from human nature. We are no longer in the climate of tragedy, where human beings themselves are seen as animals, like the Spartan dog Iago or the wolfish daughters of Lear. Though he gives a hint of reformation at the end, Caliban, in Prospero's eyes, is unimprovable; he cannot be tamed by reason; he is

> A devil, a born devil, on whose nature
> Nurture will never stick; on whom my pains
> Humanely taken, are all lost, quite lost. (IV. i. 188)

And it is characteristic of him that he should take Stephano, the lowest available specimen of human nature, for a god.

The human beings on Prospero's island are a various crew, perhaps deliberately chosen to present as wide a range as possible. Stephano and Trinculo are Shakespeare's last clowns, representing the laughable, amorally lovable, and quite unchangeable level of human nature; they are appropriately associated with Caliban. Antonio is the rigid, selfish schemer, an egotistic isolationist, cut off from all concerns but his own; Alonzo and Sebastian are also schemers, equally selfish but not as coldly self-centered as Antonio. There is Gonzalo, the testy and amiable official servant of goodness and order, the last of Shakespeare's old men, and there is Ferdinand, the ideal son and prince, the appropriate mate for Miranda, the "wonder" of the island who, like the heroines of the other last plays, is a symbol of unspoilt humanity. Most of these people, with the important and significant exception of the worst and the best, go through some kind of punishment or purgation. The low characters, Stephano and Trinculo, are merely punished, physically: they get befouled and belabored, as is appropriate—the stuff they are made of must be beaten into shape, it lacks the deeper awareness necessary for purgation. But the courtly figures, Alonzo, Antonio, and Sebastian, *are* subjected to purgation. They lose their human faculties for a time, their brains are useless, "boiled" within their skulls; "ignorant fumes . . . mantle their clearer reason," until finally

> their understanding
> Begins to swell, and the approaching tide
> Will shortly fill the reasonable shores
> That now lie foul and muddy. (V. i. 79 ff.)

And Alonzo, if not Antonio, is cured by the process. His reason having returned, he resigns the dukedom, entreating Prospero to pardon his wrongs. It is at this point that Miranda and Ferdinand are discovered, and we forget that not all of mankind is regenerate as we hear Miranda's

> How beauteous mankind is! O brave new world,
> That has such people in't!

Prospero, until he drowns his book, is clearly on a level above that of ordinary human nature, and though it would be an error to think of him as a representative of purely intellectual capacity, his use of magic is a way of making his superiority dramatically effective; the elves and demi-puppets that have been his agents were considered in certain contemporary circles of thought to be creatures above man in the hierarchy of Nature, between men and angels.[1] Prospero's command of them obviously involves a more than human power. Yet Prospero gives up this power and returns to the human level again. He is purged, but his purgation is exactly opposite to the purgation of Alonzo: Alonzo sinks *below* reason before returning to it; before Prospero returns to the rational human level he has lived for a time *above* it. The important thing to notice is his return. I cannot agree with those critics who say that Prospero at the end of the play, "finds himself immeasurably nearer than before to the impassivity of the gods." "His theurgical operations," says Mr. Curry, "have accomplished their purpose. He wishes now to take the final step and to consummate the assimilation of his soul to the gods. And this step is to be accomplished through prayer." [2]

But this is clearly a misinterpretation of Shakespeare's meaning. Prospero abjures his magic not to become like the gods, but to return to humanity:

---

[1] See W. C. Curry, *Shakespeare's Philosophical Patterns,* Baton Rouge, 1937, p. 194.

[2] *Op. cit.,* p. 196. In support of this view, Mr. Curry, like Mr. Middleton Murry, interprets Prospero's epilogue in religious terms:

> Now I want
> Spirits to enforce, art to enchant;
> And my ending is despair,
> Unless I be reliev'd by prayer,
> Which pierces so that it assaults
> Mercy itself and frees all faults.
> As you from crimes would pardon'd be,
> Let your indulgence set me free.

But the prayer is obviously merely a prayer to the audience. It is conventional for an actor to step half out of character in an epilogue, and that is what Prospero is doing here. His "prayer" consists of the last two lines, and has no metaphysical connotations.

> I will discase me, and myself present,
> As I was sometime Milan.

He compares (V. i. 170) Alonzo's "content" at his rediscovery of
Ferdinand to his own content at being restored to his dukedom, and
in fact much of the point of the play is lost if we do not see Prospero
returning to worldly responsibility. He must be restored to his position
in the state, as he must be restored to his position as a human being;
he has come to the conclusion that, though he can wreak supernatural
havoc on his enemies,

> the rarer action is
> In virtue than in vengeance,

and, his domination of the spirits having been outside the limits of
human nature, his wisdom makes him return to his rightful place as
a governor of himself, and as a governor, through his dukedom, of
other human beings as well. Prospero, on his enchanted island, has
been like a god, controlling the world of nature and the elements:

> I have bedimm'd
> The noontide sun, call'd forth the mutinous winds,
> And 'twixt the green sea and the azur'd vault
> Set roaring war: to the dread-rattling thunder
> Have I given fire and rifted Jove's stout oak
> With his own bolt: the strong-bas'd promontory
> Have I made shake; and by the spurs pluck'd up
> The pine and cedar: graves at my command
> Have wak'd their sleepers, op'd, and let them forth
> By my so potent art. (V. i. 41)

But he abjures his magic, and having "required Some heavenly
music" so that the courtiers may be restored to their senses—in Shakespeare's theater the music would have come from above, from the
musicians' gallery under the "heavens," which were painted with the
stars—he breaks his staff and plans to drown his book of magic
"deeper than did ever plummet sound." In the company of his fellow
men, Prospero returns to Milan.

The Tempest

by Bonamy Dobrée

So much has been written in the last few years about the plays of
Shakespeare's final phase, in a general re-interpretation which amounts
almost to rediscovery, that we are in danger of having a veil interposed
between us and whatever it is that Shakespeare may have to show. I
confess that after studying some of these, and feeling myself more and
more bewildered and inadequate, I comfort myself by reading that
admirable Dialogue of the Dead in which Fontenelle makes Æsop
and Homer talk together. You will remember that when Homer con-
gratulates Æsop upon artfully packing so much morality into his
fables, Æsop says:

> Il m'est bien doux d'être loué sur cet art, par vous qui l'avez si bien
> entendu.
>
> *Homère.* Moi? je ne m'en suis jamais piqué.
>
> *Ésope.* Quoi! n'avez-vous pas prétendu cacher de grands mistères dans vos
> Ouvrages?
>
> *Homère.* Hélas! point du tout.
>
> [It is pleasant to be praised for that art by you who have understood
> it so well.
>
> *Homer.* Me? I never prided myself on that.
>
> *Aesop.* What? Haven't you claimed to conceal great mysteries in your
> works?
>
> *Homer.* Alas, not at all.]

and so on, in entertaining elaboration. But, of course, the great work
of a great master, besides being an object in itself, is also a receptacle
for what each individual person can put into it, and will be reinter-

"The Tempest" *by Bonamy Dobrée. From* Essays and Studies, *New Series of Essays
and Studies Collected for the English Association by Arundell Esdaile (London:
John Murray, [Publishers] Ltd., 1952), Vol. 5, 13–25. Copyright held by Bonamy
Dobrée. Reprinted by permission of the author. This essay was originally delivered
as a lecture at the Collège Britannique in Paris. Translations have been added by
the editor.*

preted by every age. But recent essays upon these later dramas has made it extremely difficult for us to be absolutely honest in our own approach: because these plays, being, it is fairly safe to say, Shakespeare's deepest and perhaps final religious statement—using religion in its broadest sense as an apprehension of what life is about—that many writers have sought, and found, their own beliefs about Shakespeare in them, even their own religious beliefs, and used them to propagate their own gospels. Thus it is extremely hard for us to see the object as it really is—for ourselves. Only too often with these plays, the criticism of others, instead of removing barriers as it should, merely interposes fresh ones.

Nevertheless there are certain broad statements we can make, and the first is that *The Tempest* cannot be considered apart from the other three of this phase, *Pericles, Cymbeline,* and, to my mind the greatest of all these miracles, *The Winter's Tale.* To state their scope briefly I cannot do better than quote Professor Kenneth Muir:

> It is impossible to doubt that the form of the last plays was determined by [I would prefer to say adapted to] the new vision which Shakespeare wished to express. The centre of this vision was a belief in the necessity for forgiveness, the conviction that "the rarer action is in virtue than in vengeance." As Murry suggests, Shakespeare had realized, as Tchekov was later to do, that "since we are forgiven it would be strange not to forgive." The other characteristics of the plays of the last period arise from this necessity of forgiveness. Without love forgiveness is meaningless: and with forgiveness must come the reconciliation of the estranged, the restoration of the lost, the regeneration of the natural and sinful man, the birth that is a symbol of rebirth, and the conquest of death by the acceptance of the fact of death.

This is an excellent compaction of the themes: but you will have noticed that it doesn't quite fit *The Tempest,* especially as he adds "These things take time." And it does not quite fit because also—and this is the thesis I would like later to develop tentatively—Shakespeare was moving on from those themes to others, which might perhaps tacitly include these, but would be different from them. There can be no doubt, however, that *The Tempest* is closely linked with this group which is concerned with a loss or losses which seem to be death, with repentance, followed by reconciliation (after a "recognition" scene), and by forgiveness, with, as Mr. Muir also says, the sins of the fathers being healed by the children. Besides containing a very unusual number of ideas adumbrated in other plays, its structure shows more plainly than any other of Shakespeare's dramas, the storm or tempest as a symbol of turmoil with music as the healing, harmonizing influence, a structure which Mr. Wilson Knight[1] pointed out so convincingly and so long ago, that we tend to accept it, unacknowledged, as a commonplace.

But though the play belongs to this group, and is sometimes hailed as the most perfect of them all, I for one do not feel that the old intuitions have the old force: it seems to me that the poignancy of loss, and repentance, reconciliation, or forgiveness—call it grace if you like— were more convincingly brought home in the other plays, certainly in *The Winter's Tale.* I would like to suggest that the treatment of the old themes of this group is a little perfunctory. For instance, is there not a somewhat nasty taste about the quality of Prospero's forgiveness? Is it not Senecan, rather than Christian? "It is the part of a great mind to despise injuries," Seneca says in his essay on anger; "and it is one kind of revenge to neglect a man as not worth it." This seems to me exactly Prospero's sentiment with regard to Alonso. It is Ariel who has to remind him of pity and tenderness, and even then Prospero appeals to his "nobler reason," and rather priggishly performs what he thinks is a "rarer" action. And after all, it is easy enough to forgive your enemies when you have triumphed over them. When he speaks to Antonio, he may use the *word* forgiveness, but does he feel the emotion?

> For you, most wicked sir, whom to call brother
> Would even infect my mouth, I do forgive
> Thy rankest faults—all of them; and require
> My dukedom of thee, which perforce I know,
> Thou must restore.

Does that sound like forgiveness? Is that how you would speak to a man whom you love as you forgive him? Nor can it be said that any of the three men of sin—Alonso, Sebastian, and Antonio—repent. What happens to them is that they are frightened out of their wits by Ariel's speech at the banquet. The most that Gonzalo can say is:

> All three of them are desperate: their great guilt
> Like poison given to work a great time after,
> Now 'gins to bite the spirits:

and even that is only words. For Alonso feels not repentance, but regret, because his action has lost him his son. As for Sebastian, he says he'll fight hard—one fiend at a time—and Antonio says he'll second him. There is only stubbornness there. Repentance and forgive-

---

[1] *The Shakespearian Tempest,* London, 1932.

ness seem to remain as fossils in the play, rather than as active principles. Loss and recovery certainly are there in Alonso's and Ferdinand's loss of each other; the sins of the fathers are redeemed by the
children: those themes are fully stated, especially the last. But yet,
with how much less power than in the other plays, with less rapturous
poetry! I would ask you to compare the love speeches which Ferdinand
addresses to Miranda with those which burst from Florizel as he woos
Perdita. The former have amazement, but they lack warmth.

Or take one more difference between this play and the others, which
if this were really of the same sort, would make it a much weaker play:
I mean the great flower-pieces, such a marked feature in the other
three. Let me remind you just of the one in *The Winter's Tale:*

> . . . Daffodils
> That come before the swallow dares, and take
> The winds of March with beauty; violets dim
> But sweeter than the lids of Juno's eyes
> Or Cytherea's breath; pale primroses
> That die unmarried ere they can behold
> Bright Phoebus in his strength,—a malady
> Most incident to maids; bold oxlips and
> The Crown imperial; lilies of all kinds,
> The flower de luce being one. . . .

What do we get in *The Tempest?* All we find in the body of the play
is Prospero's remark to the elves:

> you demi-puppets, that
> By moonshine do the green-sour ringlets make,
> Whereof the ewe not bites: and you whose pastime
> Is to make midnight mushrumps . . .

a somewhat grim and sterile vision. And in the Masque all we get is a
strictly utilitarian catalogue—wheat, rye, barley, vetches, oats, and
pease—from Iris; and from Ceres some lines about barns and garners,
and plants with goodly burden bowing: all very proper for a fertility
rite, such as the Masque was, but this is not the passionate adoration
of the loveliness of nature. Unless we accept the postulate of a bored
and wearied Shakespeare—and therefore think the play a failure (and
it is emphatically not a failure)—we must assume that Shakespeare
was not writing about the sort of thing he had embodied in the other
plays of the group.

And if this group has also as one of its themes the regeneration of
natural and sinful man, what are we to make of Caliban whom those
who think in this way regard as the only too sinful and natural man?

For the moral of the story—if the story must have a moral—is that he cannot be regenerated: he is

> A devil, a born devil, on whose nature
> Nurture can never stick:

he must be kept in order by being hunted, pinched, tortured with cramps. True, he says at the end, when ordered to tidy up Prospero's bedroom—"I will be wise hereafter and seek for grace"—because he realizes he was a fool to follow a god with a bottle. We are not impressed. Again, the natural man in Ferdinand, apparently, can be kept in check only by threats: Prospero warns him against pre-nuptial love in words which suggest Lear's curse of sterility upon Goneril. This may have been to please James I; but what Shakespeare seems to be suggesting—or at least Prospero suggests here and in other places—is that the natural instincts have constantly to be disciplined, scourged, whipped: they cannot be integral to regenerated man. It is true that Ferdinand brings in a somewhat sweeter atmosphere by saying that nothing will ever turn his honour into lust, but that does little to freshen the general impression made by Prospero's scolding.

If I have taken you with me so far, you will conclude that though *The Tempest* is closely related to the other three plays—*Pericles, Cymbeline, The Winter's Tale*—it cannot be grouped with them; it is not a symbol of the same sort of attitude, of sentiment about life, which infuses and informs the other plays. What I would like to suggest is, that though to a large extent Shakespeare felt the mood of those other plays, he was no longer dominated by it, and was moving on to other things. He is not denying the intuitions of the other plays, but having expressed them he was not, as artist, interested in them so wholly as before: they are there, but perfunctorily stated, and a little flatly, as the background from which something else is emerging, to modify what he said earlier. But the play is so extraordinarily complex, and exists on so many levels, and what may seem important on one level scarcely exists on another.

But—and I would like to stress this—we must not forget that we are, after all, judging a stage play to which an audience could not be expected to come with their minds stored with the author's previous work. And it seems to me, that together with so much richness, certain themes are emerging which had not previously been very evident, and that these tend to thrust into the background the themes common to the group of late plays: and these are, destiny, the nature of reality, and, as Mr. Muir stresses, freedom. I, for my part, do not want to lay too much stress on these elements, especially the first, that of destiny: all I want to affirm is that they are parts of a very complex whole, and that by treating them a little separately we may be able to account for certain aspects of the play which if it is considered as one of the same sort as, shall we say, *The Winter's Tale,* appear as blemishes.

But before going on to discuss the themes themselves, I would like to touch upon the problem of stage illusion which all this group of plays offer in an acute form. They are, of course, utterly unrealistic poetic drama; the suspension of our disbelief must be practised constantly and whole-heartedly. In this play particularly, we have to accept, to live in, so to speak, another dimension of time. Let me give one instance. I read in an article the other day (Mr. Traversi in *Scrutiny,* June 1949) that, by the beginning of Act III, the sufferings of Ferdinand and Miranda had cemented their devotion. Now devotion implies a certain length of time, so that realistically that is absurd. They had known each other for about an hour and a half, and their suffering had been of the slightest: even Ferdinand's grief for his father had been promptly put aside. Yet we may find that the statement fits in without notion of what the play, at least to some extent, is about. We accept the fresh reality. But Shakespeare knew that you cannot stretch fantasy too far; so from the very beginning gave his audience the security of an intellectual setting they were familiar with —nothing so strange as ancient Tyre or Roman Britain or Illyria— but, on an island such as was being discovered every day, a sort of Bermuda, the familiar figure of the magus. As the late Professor Kittredge wrote:

> Prosper, to the Elizabethan audience, was as comprehensible in his feats of magic as a chemist or an electrical engineer is to us moderns . . . [Prospero] belonged not only to a conceivable category among men, but to an established category.

Just as Marlowe in Faustus had presented a necromancer who dealt in black magic, a being his audience perfectly understood, so here in Prospero is one dealing in white magic, as did in actual life Shakespeare's contemporary, Dr. John Dee. Prospero was, in the manner of Dr. John Dee—but, we imagine, far more effectively—controlling certain forces of nature.

In this setting, with this magus, nothing that can happen on this island is incomprehensible: even Ariel is a natural force—his name is common in charms and invocations of the time. This then is a realistic story, not a fairy-tale such as *Midsummer Night's Dream*: it is not on such obvious ground as that that Shakespeare is to discuss reality and unreality. Caliban, again, is not the sort of monster the Jacobeans would regard as an invented or fantastic figure: travellers' tales of wild men of this sort went on down to well into the eighteenth century. Thus in a sense this play would be easier to "believe"—as one believes stage plays—than any of the other three. What I am trying to suggest is, that here Shakespeare was giving himself as solid a framework as he could so as to have within it the maximum of freedom possible.

And with what amazing nimbleness he moves from one plane of reality to another (I am adopting Dr. Tillyard's expression), first of all, from one set of people to the opposite one, from the upper classes to the lower (to put it that way), which, seeing what they are, is no small feat. For the upper classes—especially Ferdinand, Miranda, Gonzalo, and Alonso (more about Prospero soon) correspond with what Mr. T. S. Eliot has said about the characters in the romances, as being "the work of a writer who has finally seen through the dramatic action of men into a spiritual action which transcends it"; but the more materialistic people, Caliban, Stephano, Trinculo, and the sailors have all the outward dramatic solidity of Shakespeare's usual figures, while Antonio and Sebastian form a link between. There is a delightful and rich earthiness about the lower group—the poet among them being Caliban—and base as they are, they are drawn with the loving realism which makes all Shakespeare's children of the lower nature so immensely likeable. Antonio and Sebastian are too puppet-like to be of any interest, as they had to be lest they should become too interesting: but when we move to the upper group the figures, as realistic figures, are pallid in the extreme. They are the dullest *jeune premier* and *jeune première:* Ferdinand is a very ordinary nice young man; the insipid young chit of fifteen that Miranda is can hardly interest us on the page (however much she might stir us in life or in the theatre). Even Prospero cannot let pass her remark "Oh brave new world that has such people in it," seeing that the people she is mainly referring to are the three men of sin: he has to say a little acidly " 'Tis new to thee"—which, incidentally, shows how far Prospero believed in "regeneration"! The "upper" characters, in short, live on an utterly different plane of reality from the "lower" ones: but this is only a sort of outer case in which the theme of the real and unreal is contained.

For the one which Shakespeare is toying with—I don't think it is more than that at this stage—is "What is reality? Is it something that we can judge of by the evidence of our senses?" The ultimate form of this question, which is touched upon only in Prospero's cloud cap'd towers speech, may be "Is there a quite different reality behind experience?" But short of that question, Shakespeare seems to be inducing in us this sense of the unreal to give a shimmering effect to this curious and delightful object he offers us: it gives us that peculiar sense of detachment which it seems to be one of his objects to achieve

—if an effect on his audience was, as he wrote, at all in his mind.
Every now and again the people in the play are deluded as to what
they see, or see only what they wish to see, or even see what is not
there. All the time there is a suggestion of unreality, of living in a
dream world. Miranda, for example, saw the ship sink—and so, it
turns out later, did the rest of the fleet: the garments of the shipwrecked people are fresher than before, in spite of their drenching in
the sea (it is true that there had to be some explanation on the realistic plane!); there is constantly a mysterious music—Ferdinand cannot
tell whether it be in the air or the earth, and soon his spirits "as in a
dream are all bound up," spell-bound by Prospero. Or take the little
passage near the beginning of the second act:

> *Adrian.* The air breathes upon us here most sweetly.
> *Sebastian.* As if it had lungs, and rotten ones.
> *Antonio.* Or, as 'twere perfumed by a fan.
> *Gonzalo.* How lush and lusty the grass looks! how green!
> *Antonio.* The ground, indeed, is tawny.
> *Sebastian.* With an eye of green in't.

Which is right in their sense of reality? Is not each making his own
according to his temperament? "The quality o' the climate" makes
some drowsy and the spirit of others more active. Caliban lives in a
world inhabited by spirits, and for him the island is full of noises,
some of them ravishing, while Ariel causes the utmost confusion in the
conversation of Caliban with Stephano and Trinculo. At the end
Gonzalo is utterly astray between the real and the unreal: as Prospero
tells him

> You do yet taste
> Some subtilties o' th' isle, that will not let you
> Believe things certain,

while Alonso fears that the Ferdinand whom he sees may prove "a
vision of the island."

All the while the shimmer is there, quite apart from the scenes of
magic, the banquet which vanishes, the appearance of Ariel as a
harpy, the masque, with all the attendant bewilderments, out of which
arises Prospero's great philosophic speech. It is true that in the Earl
of Stirling's *Tragedy of Darius* Shakespeare had read

> . . . let this worldly pomp our wits inchant
> All fades and scarcely leaves behind a token . . .
> Those stately Courts, those sky-encountering walls
> Evanish all like vapours in the air

but if Shakespeare borrowed a little of the imagery, the thought is a commonplace made actual and vivid, a truth imaginatively grasped by the power of the poetry of a man who for the moment at least felt it all with the assent of an intuition. The whole sense of insubstantiality is there, one that all of us have probably felt at some time or another with varying keenness. All of us feel sometimes, perhaps hope, that we are such stuff as dreams are made on, and welcome the relief of thinking that our little lives are rounded with a sleep. Thus for a certain part of our apprehension the play gathers momentum up to this point, and after that flows away from it.

But for a certain part only, for interwoven with the theme is one almost contrary, since Fate and destiny can hardly be said to apply to shadows; yet the theme is there. In the very first scene Gonzalo says of the boatswain: "Stand fast, good Fate, to his hanging, make the rope of his destiny our cable," a jesting reference, yes: but the words are there to make an impact on our consciousness. This is somewhat waveringly supported in the next scene. It was "Providence divine"— which we may equate with destiny—that had brought Prospero and Miranda ashore; and then we learn that "bountiful Fortune" (not of course chance, in our sense, but the inescapable Wheel of Fortune familiar to the mediæval mind) had brought Prospero's enemies to the island; and Prospero tells Miranda that

> by my prescience
> I find my zenith doth depend upon
> A most auspicious star, whose influence
> If now I court not, but omit, my fortunes
> Will ever after droop:

Antonio next, when egging Sebastian on to murder, appeals somewhat confusedly to destiny. But of course, the grand statement comes in the speech Ariel makes when as a harpy he sweeps away the feast offered to the bewildered travellers. It is phrased with very special power, placed so that we cannot but notice it:

> You are three men of sin, whom destiny,
> That hath to instrument this lower world
> And what is in't, the never-surfeited sea
> Hath caused to belch up . . .

It is curious, by the way, that Ariel uses some of the coarsest imagery in the play, Caliban some of the most etherial; but that is another issue. Ariel goes on:

> . . . . You fools! I and my fellows
> Are ministers of fate,

and later he informs the men of sin that:

> The powers delaying, not forgetting, have
> Incensed the seas and shores—yea, all the creatures
> Against your peace.

So the idea is stated—not indeed very emphatically, since we, the audience, knowing that Ariel is pretending, play-acting, speaking the part Prospero told him to. Nevertheless something has happened in our minds; and perhaps when Ferdinand a little later says that Miranda is his "by immortal Providence," we may be a little inclined to believe him, though we know that it came about largely by Prospero's contrivance. The element must not, I think, be stressed; but it is there.

The last thread, that of freedom, is more insistent. It runs through the whole of the Ariel part, as I need not remind you; again and again he asks when he shall be free; again and again Prospero promises him his freedom. We are never allowed to forget it. At first, with Caliban, we hear of the opposite: he is "slave Caliban." But he has his aspirations: one of the notes in the play that everyone remembers is his

> 'Ban 'Ban, Ca-Caliban
> Has a new master—get a new man.
> Freedom, high-day! high-day, freedom! freedom, high-day, freedom!

as he leads Stephano and Trinculo to a happier state of life. Poor wretch, prototype here, perhaps, of the wretchedest mob, incapable of scepticism and so always deluded, believing ever that a change of masters will mean greater freedom for the man, and ever disillusioned. That interpretation need not detain us. Ferdinand, who tells us early (a romantic commonplace)

> Might I but through my prison once a day
> Behold this maid, all corners else o' th' earth
> Let liberty make use of, space enough
> Have I in such a prison

later finds freedom in the service of Miranda. The play ends with the idea of freedom, of release (the opposite, we note, of Fate or Destiny), with Prospero saying to Ariel, "Be free and fare thou well:"—the last line of the epilogue which cannot but ring in our ears, being

> Let your indulgence set me free.

That then ends the play, composed throughout so musically, with a lovely diaphaneity of verse scarcely distinguishable from the beautifully flexible prose, itself almost verse, that gives a kind of iridescent effect to this gracious object: and what I want to suggest is that in it

Shakespeare was using for fundamental material, not so much the moral intuitions of repentance, forgiveness, reconciliation, and so on, but the metaphysical intuitions of fate and freedom, of appearance and reality. Perhaps that is what Mr. Eliot meant. And out of these he spun the enchanting fable, a kind of transparent object which, if we will let it, may set, us also, a little more free.

But is there not more? the question will be asked. Have we not here in Prospero, Shakespeare himself taking his farewell of the stage? I fear that some confusion has been caused by this ingenious conjecture, born some two hundred years after the play was acted. Perhaps as he wrote some of the passages a certain metaphorical resemblance between him and Prospero struck him whimsically, and he developed it a little, especially in the notorious farewell passage, which was a piece of common material about magicians he took almost verbatim from some lines in Golding's Ovid,[2] and, as usual transformed. Surely he would not have wished the likeness pushed too closely, in view of what Prospero is—a philosopher King, who like his prototype in *Measure for Measure* was a disastrous ruler; a somewhat cruel, uncertain-tempered man, who far from renouncing anything, was going back to the enjoyment of worldly greatness; so we should not be pressed to regard the play as a kind of last will and testament, especially as Shakespeare did not break his wand or drown his book: (*Henry VIII* followed, at least largely his, and portions of *Two Noble Kinsmen*). I admit it is possible that he had solved his problems on the plane of ordinary living, that he no longer wanted to write as he had done, and that he was moving into realms where he was finding, as Rimbaud was to find, that *paroles païennes* would not express what now he had to say. However, all that may be, I do not believe he was writing a kind of valedictory sermon; but that he was doing what every artist does in every work, exploring reality, here, in some ways, almost directly, and expressing the inapprehensible in symbols which he hoped might bring him illumination.

Nothing more definite? Alas! I hear once more the voice of Æsop, speaking to Homer:

> Tous les savants de mon temps . . . soutenaient que tous les secrets de la théologie, de la physique, de la morale, et des mathématiques même, étaient renfermés dans ce que vous aviez écrit. Véritablement il y avait quelque difficulté à les développer: où l'un trouvait un sens moral, l'autre en trouvait un physique: mais après cela ils convenaient que vous aviez tout su, et tout dit à qui le comprenait bien.
>
> [All the critics of my time maintain that all the secrets of theology,

[2] VII. 192–219.

of physics, of morals, even of mathematics, were wrapped up in your
writings. Truly there was a certain difficulty in unfolding them: where
one critic found a moral meaning, another found a physical, but after
all they agreed that you knew everything and revealed it to whoever
could understand.]

And indeed there have not been lacking those (*qui le comprenaient
bien*) to tell us what *The Tempest* is really about—from those who
would have it that Shakespeare was writing so rigid a thing as an
allegory, to those whose delicacy of perception delights us, helps our
own imagination, leads us to follow threads which promise to lead
us excitedly to the centre of the maze. It may be, as Mr. Robert Graves
tells us,[3] that

> in one aspect *The Tempest* is a play of revenge on [Shakespeare's] per-
> sonal enemies, that in another it is his farewell to the stage, in another a
> political satire, in another a religious mystery, in another a spectacle to
> please the common people, in another a celebration of a royal wedding,
> in another a piece of rhythmic music—all these are legitimate aspects,
> but . . .

Indeed yes, but . . . Let us pull ourselves up, even perhaps a little
sharply, and desist from pursuing these threads. I do not think that
in dissecting a work of art we murder it, but it is possible that we
may not be such skilful anatomists as we would like to think. We
may, of course, extract such morals as we see fit from any work of art,
but I cannot regard *The Tempest* as a sermon, nor believe that
Shakespeare was engaged in delivering what M. de Norpois would
describe as "*un véritable prêchis-prêchas.*" And if in the deliciously
neat, humorous, and perhaps deeply felt epilogue Prospero really is
Shakespeare, what was it from which he was praying to be set free?
May it not have been from what Lamb called the everlasting cox-
combry of our moral pretensions? It is, certainly, always a difficult
point to determine how far a great artist is conscious of what he is
doing until he has done it; like the rest of us (indeed more so) he must
say to himself in the now common phrase which I think M. André
Gide invented: "How can I know what I mean till I see what I say?"
What, as I believe, the poet does, is, by giving us a thing of delight,
to release our spirits into a world of conjecture, freed of any immediate necessity for action. His materials are the thoughts, impulses,
velleities which at the moment most occupy him; his symbols are the
people he offers to our view, what happens to them, and the music of
his utterance. The difference between works of art, in their importance,
is the difference in the kind of realm into which we are released, to

[3] *Poetic Unreason*, London, 1925, p. 232.

ponder and to muse, the degree of sensitive awareness induced in us. If we allow "the meddling intellect," as Wordsworth called it, to meddle too curiously, we prevent the work of art from giving us what it might. We are forcing it, submitting it to our lesser purposes. Surely we should apply Blake's warning:

> He who binds to himself a joy
> Does the wingèd life destroy:
> But he who kisses the joy as it flies
> Lives in eternity's sunrise.

So let us be a little delicate with this lovely thing which Shakespeare gave us, a thing composed of the impulses of love and forgiveness, of fear, of the sense of destiny, of the immateriality of our existence, of the brutality of matter; composed with grace of movement to the sound of entrancing music, a music sometimes terrible, sometimes miraculously sweet, but which brings the whole into a harmony which lies beyond contradiction. The lesson? Well, perhaps there is a lesson: but art, as De Quincey said,[4] "can teach only as nature teaches, as forests teach, as the sea teaches, as infancy teaches, namely by deep impulse, by hieroglyphic suggestion." Maybe we do it wrong to offer it a show of violence in trying to extract secrets from it, the secrets it might reveal if we fitted it less into our preconceptions, and let it quietly do its work upon us. For

> . . . Who in his own backyard
> Has not opened his heart to the smiling
> Secret he cannot quote?
> Which goes to show that the Bard
> Was sober when he wrote
> That this world of fact we love
> Is unsubstantial stuff!
> All the rest is silence
> On the other side of the wall;
> And the silence ripeness,
> And the ripeness all.[5]

[4] Speaking of Pope and didacticism.

[5] W. H. Auden. *The Sea and the Mirror*. Quoted by kind permission of the author and Messrs. Faber and Faber, Ltd.

Introduction to *The Tempest*

by Northrop Frye

In the opening scene of *The Tempest* there is not only a sinking ship but a dissolving society. The storm, like the storm in *King Lear*, does not care that it is afflicting a king, and Gonzalo's protests about the deference due to royalty seem futile enough. But while everyone is unreasonable, we can distinguish Gonzalo, who is ready to meet his fate with some detachment and humor, from Antonio and Sebastian, who are merely screaming abuse at the sailors trying to save their lives. The boatswain, who comes so vividly to life in a few crisp lines, dominates this scene and leaves us with a strong sense of the superiority of personal character to social rank.

The shipwrecked characters are then divided by Ariel into three main groups: Ferdinand; the Court Party proper; Stephano and Trinculo. Each goes through a pursuit of illusions, an ordeal, and a symbolic vision. The Court Party hunts for Ferdinand with strange shapes appearing and vanishing around them; their ordeal is a labyrinth of "forthrights and meanders" in which they founder with exhaustion, and to them is presented the vision of the disappearing banquet, symbolic of deceitful desires. There follows confinement and a madness which brings them to conviction of sin, self-knowledge, and repentance. Like Hamlet, Prospero delays revenge and sets up a dramatic action to catch the conscience of a king; like Lear on a small scale, Alonso is a king who gains in dignity by suffering. The search of Stephano and Trinculo for Prospero is also misled by illusions; their ordeal is a horsepond and their symbolic vision the "trumpery" dangled in front of them. What happens to them is external and physical rather than internal and mental: they are hunted by hounds, filled with cramps, and finally reach what might be called a conviction of inadequacy. Probably they then settle into their old roles again: if a cold-blooded sneering assassin like Antonio can be forgiven, these

From "Introduction" by Northrop Frye. From The Tempest *(Baltimore: Penguin Books, Inc., 1959), pp. 15–26. Copyright © 1959 by Penguin Books, Inc. Reprinted by permission of the publisher.*

amusing and fundamentally likeable rascals can be too. Ferdinand, being the hero, has a better time: he is led by Ariel's music to Miranda, undergoes the ordeal of the log-pile, where he takes over Caliban's role as a bearer of wood, and his symbolic vision is that of the wedding masque.

The characters thus appear to be taking their appropriate places in a new kind of social order. We soon realize that the island looks different to different people—it is a pleasanter place to Gonzalo than to Antonio or Sebastian—and that each one is stimulated to exhibit his own ideal of society. At one end, Ferdinand unwillingly resigns himself to becoming King of Naples by the death of Alonso; at the other, Sebastian plots to become King of Naples by murdering Alonso. In between come Stephano, whose ambition to be king of the island is more ridiculous but somehow less despicable than Sebastian's, and Gonzalo, who dreams of a primitive golden age of equality and leisure, not very adequate as a social theory, but simple and honest, full of good nature and good will, like Gonzalo himself.

Into the midst of this society comes the islander Caliban, who is, on one level of nature, a natural man, a primitive whose name seems to echo the "cannibals" of Montaigne's famous essay. He is not a cannibal, but his existence in the play forms an ironic comment on Gonzalo's reverie, which has been taken from a passage in the same essay. Caliban is a human being, as Ariel is not; and whatever he does, Prospero feels responsible for him: "This thing of darkness I Acknowledge mine," Prospero says. Whether or not he is, as one hopeful critic suggested, an anticipation of Darwin's "missing link," he knows he is not like the apes "with foreheads villainous low"; his sensuality is haunted by troubled dreams of beauty; he is not taken in by the "trumpery," and we leave him with his mind on higher things. His ambitions are to kill Prospero and rape Miranda, both, considering his situation, eminently natural desires; and even these he resigns to Stephano, to whom he tries to be genuinely loyal. Nobody has a good word for Caliban: he is a born devil to Prospero, an abhorred slave to Miranda, and to others not obviously his superiors either in intelligence or virtue he is a puppy-headed monster, a mooncalf, and a plain fish. Yet he has his own dignity, and he is certainly no Yahoo, for all his ancient and fishlike smell. True, Shakespeare, like Swift, clearly does not assume that the natural man on Caliban's level is capable also of a reasonable life. But he has taken pains to make Caliban as memorable and vivid as any character in the play.

As a natural man, Caliban is *mere* nature, nature without nurture, as Prospero would say: the nature that manifests itself more as an instinctive propensity to evil than as the calculated criminality of

Antonio and Sebastian, which is rationally corrupted nature. But to an Elizabethan poet "nature" had an upper level, a cosmic and moral order that may be entered through education, obedience to law, and the habit of virtue. In this expanded sense we may say that the whole society being formed on the island under Prospero's guidance is a natural society. Its top level is represented by Miranda, whose chastity and innocence put her, like her poetic descendant the Lady in *Comus,* in tune with the harmony of a higher nature. The discipline necessary to live in this higher nature is imposed on the other characters by Prospero's magic. In Shakespeare's day the occult arts, especially alchemy, whose language Prospero is using at the beginning of the fifth act, were often employed as symbols of such discipline.

Shakespeare did not select Montaigne's essay on the cannibals as the basis for Gonzalo's "commonwealth" speech merely at random. Montaigne is no Rousseau: he is not talking about imaginary noble savages. He is saying that, despite their unconventional way of getting their proteins, cannibals have many virtues we have not, and if we pretend to greater virtues we ought to have at least theirs. They are not models for imitation; they are children of nature who can show us what is unnatural in our own lives. If we can understand that, we shall be wiser than the cannibals as well as wiser than our present selves. Prospero takes the society of Alonso's ship, immerses it in magic, and then sends it back to the world, its original ranks restored, but given a new wisdom in the light of which Antonio's previous behavior can be seen to be "unnatural." In the Epilogue Prospero hands over to the audience what his art has created, a vision of a society permeated by the virtues of tolerance and forgiveness, in the form of one of the most beautiful plays in the world. And, adds Prospero, you might start practising those virtues by applauding the play.

The Tempest is not an allegory, or a religious drama: if it were, Prospero's great "revels" speech would say, not merely that all earthly things will vanish, but that an eternal world will take their place. In a religious context, Prospero's renunciation of magic would represent the resigning of his will to a divine will, one that can do what the boatswain says Gonzalo cannot do, command the elements to silence and work the peace of the present. In Christianity the higher level of nature is God's original creation, from which man broke away with Adam's fall. It is usually symbolized by the music of the heavenly spheres, of which the one nearest us is the moon. The traditional conception of the magician was of one who could control the moon: this power is attributed to Sycorax, but it is a sinister power, and is not associated with Prospero, whose magic and music belong to the sublunary world.

In the wedding masque of the fourth act and the recognition scene of the fifth, therefore, we find ourselves moving, not out of the world, but from an ordinary to a renewed and ennobled vision of nature. The masque shows the meeting of a fertile earth and a gracious sky introduced by the goddess of the rainbow, and leads up to a dance of nymphs representing the spring rains with reapers representing the autumnal harvest. The masque has about it the freshness of Noah's new world, after the tempest had receded and the rainbow promised that seedtime and harvest should not cease. There is thus a glimpse, as Ferdinand recognizes, of an Earthly Paradise where, as in Milton's Eden, there is no winter but spring and autumn "Danced hand in hand." In the last act, as in *The Winter's Tale,* there is a curious pretense that some of the characters have died and are brought back to life. The discovery of Ferdinand is greeted by Sebastian, of all people, as "a most high miracle." But the miracles are those of a natural, and therefore also a moral and intellectual, renewal of life. Some of Shakespeare's romances feature a final revelation through a goddess or oracle, both of which Alonso expects, but in *The Tempest* goddess and oracle are represented by Miranda and Ariel (in his speech at the banquet) respectively. Ariel is a spirit of nature, and Miranda is a natural spirit, in other words a human being, greeting the "brave new world" in all the good faith of innocence.

Hence we distort the play if we think of Prospero as supernatural, just as we do if we think of Caliban as a devil. Prospero is a tempest-raiser like the witches in *Macbeth,* though morally at the opposite pole; he is a "white" magician. Anyone with Prospero's powers is an agent of fate, a cheating fate if evil, a benevolent fate or providence if motivated as he is. Great courage was required of all magicians, white or black, for the elemental spirits they controlled were both unwilling and malignant, and any sign of faltering meant terrible disaster. Ariel is loyal because of his debt of gratitude to Prospero, and because he is a very high-class spirit, too delicate to work for a black witch like Sycorax. But even he has a short memory, and has to be periodically reminded what his debt of gratitude is. Of the others Caliban says, probably with some truth, "They all do hate him As rootedly as I." The nervous strain of dealing with such creatures shows up in Prospero's relations with human beings too; and in his tormenting of Caliban, in his lame excuse for making Ferdinand's wooing "uneasy," in his fussing over protecting Miranda from her obviously honorable lover, there is a touch of the busybody.

Still, his benevolence is genuine, and as far as the action of the play goes he seems an admirable ruler. Yet he appears to have been a remarkably incompetent Duke of Milan, and not to be promising much improvement after he returns. His talents are evidently dramatic rather than political, and he seems less of a practical magician plotting the discomfiture of his enemies than a creative artist calling spirits from their confines to enact his present fancies. It has often been thought that Prospero is a self-portrait of Shakespeare, and there may well be something in him of a harassed, overworked actor-manager, scolding the lazy actors, praising the good ones in connoisseur's language, thinking up jobs for the idle, constantly aware of his limited time before his show goes on, his nerves tense and alert for breakdowns while it is going on, looking forward longingly to peaceful retirement, yet in the meantime having to go out and beg the audience for applause.

Prospero's magic, in any case, is an "art" which includes, in fact largely consists of, music and drama. Dramatists from Euripides to Pirandello have been fascinated by the paradox of reality and illusion in drama: the play is an illusion like the dream, and yet a focus of reality more intense than life affords. The action of *The Tempest* moves from sea to land, from chaos to new creation, from reality to realization. What seems at first illusory, the magic and music, becomes real, and the *Realpolitik* of Antonio and Sebastian becomes illusion. In this island the quality of one's dreaming is an index of character. When Antonio and Sebastian remain awake plotting murder, they show that they are the real dreamers, sunk in the hallucinations of greed. We find Stephano better company because his are the exuberant dreams of the stage boaster, as when he claims to have swum thirty-five leagues "off and on," when we know that he has floated to shore on a wine cask. Caliban's life is full of nightmare interspersed by strange gleams of ecstasy. When the Court Party first came to the island "no man was his own"; they had not found their "proper selves." Through the mirages of Ariel, the mops and mows of the other spirits, the vanities of Prospero's art, and the fevers of madness, reality grows up in them from inside, in response to the fertilizing influence of illusion.

Few plays are so haunted by the passing of time as *The Tempest*: it has derived even its name from a word (*tempestas*) which means time as well as tempest. Timing was important to a magician: everything depended on it when the alchemist's project gathered to a head; astrologers were exact observers of time ("The very minute bids thee ope thine ear," Prospero says to Miranda), and the most famous of all stories about magicians, the story told in Greene's play *Friar Bacon and Friar Bungay*, had the warning of "time is past" for its moral. The same preoccupation affects the other characters too, from the sailors in the storm to Ariel watching the clock for his freedom. The tide, which also waits for no man, ebbs and flows around this Mediterranean island in defiance of geography, and its imagery enters the plotting of Antonio and Sebastian and the grief of Ferdinand. When everyone is trying to make the most of his time, it seems strange that a melancholy elegy over the dissolving of all things in time should be the emotional crux of the play.

A very deliberate echo in the dialogue gives us the clue to this. Morally, *The Tempest* shows a range of will extending from Prospero's self-control, which includes his control of all the other characters, to the self-abandonment of Alonso's despair, when, crazed with guilt and grief, he resolves to drown himself "deeper than e'er plummet sounded." Intellectually, it shows a range of vision extending from the realizing of a moment in time, the zenith of Prospero's fortune, which becomes everyone else's zenith too, to the sense of the nothingness of all temporal things. When Prospero renounces his magic, his "book" falls into the vanishing world, "deeper than did ever plummet sound." He has done what his art can do; he has held the mirror up to nature. Alonso and the rest are promised many explanations after the play is over, but we are left only with the darkening mirror, the visions fading and leaving not a rack behind. Once again the Epilogue reminds us that Prospero has used up all his magic in the play, and what more he can do depends on us.

It is not difficult to see, then, why so many students of Shakespeare, rightly or wrongly, have felt that *The Tempest* is in a peculiar sense Shakespeare's play, and that there is something in it of Shakespeare's farewell to his art. Two other features of it reinforce this feeling: the fact that no really convincing general source for the play has yet been discovered, and the fact that it is probably the last play wholly written by Shakespeare.

Whether a general source turns up or not, *The Tempest* is still erudite and allusive enough, full of echoes of literature, from the classics to the pamphlets of Shakespeare's own time. The scene of the play, an island somewhere between Tunis and Naples, suggests the journey of Aeneas from Carthage to Rome. Gonzalo's identification of Tunis and Carthage, and the otherwise tedious business about "Widow Dido" in the second act, seem almost to be emphasizing the parallel. Like *The Tempest*, the *Aeneid* begins with a terrible storm and goes on to tell a story of wanderings in which a banquet with harpies figures prominently. Near the route of Aeneas' journey, according to Virgil, was the abode of Circe, of whom (at least in her Renaissance form) Sycorax is a close relative. Circe suggests Medea, whose speech in Ovid's *Metamorphoses* is the model for Prospero's renunciation speech. Echoes from the shipwreck of St. Paul (Ariel's phrase "not a hair perished" recalls Acts 27:34), from St. Augustine, who also had associations with Carthage, and from Apuleius, with his interest in magic and initiation, are appropriate enough in such a play. Most of the traditional magical names of elemental spirits were of Hebrew origin, and "Ariel," a name occurring in the Bible (Isaiah 29:1), was among them.

The imagery of contemporary accounts of Atlantic voyages has also left strong traces in *The Tempest*, and seems almost to have been its immediate inspiration. One ship of a fleet that sailed across the ocean to reinforce Raleigh's Virginian colony in 1609 had an experience rather like that of Alonso's ship. It was driven aground on the Bermudas by a storm and given up for lost, but the passengers managed to survive the winter there and reached Virginia the following spring. William Strachey's account of this experience, *True Reportory of the Wracke*, dated July 15, 1610, was not published until after Shakespeare's death, and as Shakespeare certainly knew it, he must have read it in manuscript. Strachey and a closely related pamphlet, Sylvester Jourdain's *Discovery of the Barmudas* (1610), lie behind Caliban's allusions to making dams for fish and to water with "berries" (i.e. cedarberries) in it. Other details indicate Shakespeare's reading in similar accounts. Setebos is mentioned as a god ("divell") of the Patagonians in Richard Eden's *History of Travayle in the West and East Indies* (1577), and the curious "bowgh, wawgh" refrain in Ariel's first song seems to be from a contemporary account of an Indian dance. It is a little puzzling why New World imagery should be so prominent in *The Tempest*, which really has nothing to do with the New World, beyond Ariel's reference to the "still-vexed Bermoothes" and a general, if vague, resemblance between the relation of Caliban to the other characters and that of the American Indians to the colonizers and drunken sailors who came to exterminate or enslave them.

However that may be, the dates of these pamphlets help to establish the fact that *The Tempest* is a very late play. A performance of it is recorded for November 1, 1611, in Whitehall, and it also formed part of the celebrations connected with the wedding of King James's daughter Elizabeth in the winter of 1612–13. The versification is also that of a late play, for *The Tempest* is written in the direct speaking style of Shakespeare's last period, the lines full of weak endings and so welded together that every speech is a verse paragraph in itself, often very close in its rhythm to prose, especially in the speeches of Caliban. One should read the verse as an actor would read it, attending to the natural stresses, of which there are usually four to a line, rather than the metre. Some critics have felt that a few lines are "unmetrical," but no line that can be easily spoken on the stage is unmetrical, and it is simple enough to find the four natural stresses in "You do *look*, my *son*, in a *moved sort*," or (in octosyllabics) "*Earth's in*crease, *foison* *plenty."* In such writing all the regular schematic forms of verse, rhyme, alliteration, assonance, and the like, fall into the background, peeping out irregularly through the texture:

> I will stand to, and feed;
> Although my last, no matter, since I feel
> The best is past. Brother, my lord the Duke,
> Stand to, and do as we.

In its genre *The Tempest* shows a marked affinity with dramatic forms outside the normal range of tragedy and comedy. Among these is the masque: besides containing an actual masque, *The Tempest* is like the masque in its use of elaborate stage machinery and music. The magician with his wand and mantle was a frequent figure in masques, and Caliban is like the "wild men" common in the farcical interludes known as antimasques. Another is the *commedia dell' arte,* which was well known in England. Some of the sketchy plots of this half-improvised type of play have been preserved, and they show extraordinary similarities to *The Tempest,* especially in the Stephano-Trinculo scenes. *The Tempest* in short is a spectacular and operatic play, and when we think of other plays like it, we are more apt to think of, say, Mozart's *Magic Flute* than of ordinary stage plays.

But more important than these affiliations is the position of *The Tempest* as the fourth and last of the great romances of Shakespeare's final period. In these plays Shakespeare seems to have distilled the essence of all his work in tragedy, comedy, and history, and to have reached the very bedrock of drama itself, with a romantic spectacle which is at once primitive and sophisticated, childlike and profound. In these plays the central structural principles of drama emerge with great clarity, and we become aware of the affinity between the happy endings of comedy and the rituals marking the great rising rhythms of life: marriage, spring-time, harvest, dawn, and rebirth. In *The Tempest* there is also an emphasis on moral and spiritual rebirth which suggests rituals of initiation, like baptism or the ancient mystery dramas, as well as of festivity. And just as its poetic texture ranges from the simplicity of Ariel's incredibly beautiful songs to the haunting solemnity of Prospero's speeches, so we may come to the play on any level, as a fairy tale with unusually lifelike characters, or as an inexhaustibly profound drama that has influenced some of the most complex poems in the language, including Milton's *Comus* and Eliot's *The Waste Land.* However, we take it, *The Tempest* is a play not simply to be read or seen or even studied, but possessed.

The Tempest

by Don Cameron Allen

Though *The Tempest* is a play, it is also a complicated masque or
a narrative poem with lyric intervals. It is difficult to compare with
Shakespeare's other plays, for it is briefer, more elaborate in fantasy,
and in some respects more intensely personal than they. During the
last century, it was thought to be confessional and Prospero's final
speeches were associated with Shakespeare's retirement from the
theater. The play does not permit this conclusion. Shakespeare is
not forsaking his art. If *The Tempest* is to be read biographically at
all, it must be seen as a poetical summary of the poet's life and its
satisfactory achievements, as the poetic rendering of that bright moment at the end allowed to men of special favor, a moment that assures
them that what they have loved will endure. *The Tempest,* like
Pericles, Cymbeline, and *The Winter's Tale,* is one of a series of warm
afternoons in the late autumn of Shakepeare's life. It is mellow with
the ripeness of knowledge, for its maker has discovered the right
ritual for the marriage of the inner and the outer world, of the real
and the ideal, the experienced and the imagined, the dream and the
actuality.

With the writing of *Hamlet* Shakespeare begins to experiment with
darkness, and the sun does not come again until Pericles, who is
"music's master," hears, like no other character in Shakespeare's plays,
the harmony of the heavenly spheres. This is the same harmonious
end toward which Prospero looks: "When I have required/ Some
heavenly music—which even now I do." It is plain from the tragedies
that an awakening from idealism into cold reality is the required
preliminary experience to the search for celestial harmony. The
distaste for life expressed by Hamlet, a distaste that helps to shape the
succeeding tragedies, has been associated by biographical critics with

From "The Tempest" *by Don Cameron Allen. From* Image and Meaning, Meta-
phoric Traditions in Renaissance Poetry *(Baltimore: Johns Hopkins Press, 1960),
pp. 42–52, 60–62. Copyright © 1960 by Johns Hopkins Press. Reprinted by permission of the publisher.*

the poet's private experience, with his increasing boredom with life and art, with an obsessing puritanical temper, with a disappointment in love or friendship, and with some sort of neurotic illness. None of this can be proved. All we know is that Shakespeare experimented with tragedy and tragic despair; then, using the same sets of tragic circumstances, he led his creatures out of the world of darkness into eternal day.

In each of the three plays written before *The Tempest,* the dramatic premise is tragic, although the poet always forfends "the promised end." Pericles, a Hamlet-like seeker of truth, begins his search in a place evil with the reek of incest and carnage. He wanders through storm upon storm over the wide map of the great lost world of antiquity. In the end, he hears the divine music, sees the vision of the celestial "goddess argentine," and finds at last his lost wife and child. The play follows an established legend, but the bareness of myth is made a living reality through the poet's restored belief. *Cymbeline,* which is drawn from the truth of history, shuns history so that Cymbeline may see the consequence of wrong, that Imogen may triumph in her love, that the lost princes may be found, that Posthumus, cured and forgiven, may have his dream made real, and that Iachimo, weak son of Iago, may be pardoned. With *The Winter's Tale* the miracle increases, for Greene, father of the story, could not believe in the resurrection of Hermione or the redemption of Leontes. Shakespeare, the poet, is alone able to distract the current that flows toward tragedy. The end is so miraculous that we, too, like the healed King Leontes, may say, "If this be magic, let it be an art/ Lawful as eating." The ritual of restoration, the magic that transforms the stale world into the "brave new world," is presented to us in the last play, which interprets the mode of all these romances. We must go to *The Tempest* for this information and then we may understand what the wise, young poet Keats meant when he said that Shakespeare lived the life of allegory.

The Tempest, like the other last plays, is separated from the world of the Elizabethans by an imaginative reach that is greater than the finite measurements of space and time. It is remote in time and it is out of time. The imaginative distances are enhanced by the mortal chronology of the text: the precise three hours of the action and of the twelve-year island sojourn of Prospero and Miranda. Because of these exact statements the interior distance between us and the island is closer than are the external distances of time and space. We can almost find the island in the atlas of literary tradition: it is on or off the direct course to Carthage or Tunis, the capes where Aeneas, swept by storm, came into the realm of "widow Dido." The time

may be any time, but it is more truly a constant present. All of these
distinctions are made certain by the past, for it is not just that Shakespeare was an Englishman or read the sea adventures of Jourdan that
put the island on the chart of his imagination.

We stand, at the play's beginning, watching a storm that we also
see through the eyes of Prospero, the stormmaker, and of the admirable
Miranda. It is a fairy storm, real only to the men returning from
Carthage and to the spellbound girl. It is a storm similar to the one
that Prospero may have known inwardly when twelve years before
he and his infant daughter crossed the same waters on "a rotten
carcass of a butt."

> There they hoist us,
> To cry to the seas, that roared to us; to sigh
> To the winds, whose pity sighing back again
> Did us but loving wrong.[1]

The storm that was then in Prospero's mind was not unlike the one
that drove Lear mad, but now, except for occasional ripples of anger
or impatience, it has blown itself out. Prospero has been tested and
educated in his island; he has learned to control his passions' weather
and so he can make storms in semblance. When Miranda asks how they
came ashore, Prospero, grateful for the experience, can give her a
serene answer, "By Providence divine." To reach this emotional
shelter, one must pass through stormy weather to an island, and it is
on the island, outside of known reality, that a symbolic miracle can
occur.

To come across broad waters in a helpless boat and to find haven
at last in a magic island is a symbolic motif that has found a place in
the history of heroes since literature began. The storms that drove
the Argonauts are poetically recorded;[2] we know in the same way the
wracking tumult in which Ceyx drowned[3] and the monstrous gale
that brought Aeneas to Carthage.[4] The accounts of the poets are
sustained by the romantic historians, one of whom, Diodorus Siculus,
gives us the tale of Iambulus, storm-driven for months in the Ery-
thraean Sea and brought at last to an island where men lived happily
in the earliest of Utopias.[5] The same romancer, in his book of islands,
sets down a legend congenial with that of *The Tempest*. He writes
that sailors from Carthage, exploring the sea beyond the Pillars of

[1] I. ii. 148–51.
[2] Apollonius of Rhodes, *Argonautica* IV. 1228–1304; Valerius Flaccus I. 574–607.
[3] *Metamorphoses* XI. 481–534.
[4] *Aeneid* I. 81–141.
[5] *Bibliotheca* II. 55–60.

Hercules, were carried by strong winds far into the ocean. After many
days, they were driven onto an island filled with springs, rivers, and
beautiful orchards but unknown to men. Its climate was so felicitous
that "it would appear . . . that it was a dwelling-place of gods."[6]
But the master of storm, of shipwreck, and of enchanted islands is the
wise son of Laertes, Odysseus of many counsels. To understand part
of the tradition behind *The Tempest,* we should rehearse his Mediterranean journeys and understand what they mean.

   The whole course of Odysseus from Troy to the high hall of King
Alcinous is related by Homer in the central section of the epic. It is
placed in the mouth of the great adventurer, who takes on himself
a kind of "minstrelsy" (ῥαψῳδία), as he words it, in order to offer the
listening Phaeacians his real story as a counterwork to the artful
myth recited by Demodocus. The storm begins to blow after the
boats leave the beach at Ismarus; for nine days the ruinous winds
carry the hero past Malea and Cythera to the Land of the Lotus-
Eaters. Even when the son of Hippotas gives the wanderers a wallet
containing the ways of the winds, a triumph of ill-counsel brings the
tempest again until further smash and bluster drive Odysseus with
his single ship to the island of Circe. After she frees Odysseus and his
companions and the dreaded rocks are avoided, the storms crash
again, destroying all but the hero, who is carried after nine days to
Ogygia "where dwelt Calypso of the braided hair." His release from
this island at the request of the gods and his long and stormy voyage
on the raft of his own making to the kingdom of Alcinous end the
mighty story that he relates to the king and his white-armed wife,
Arete. This is the way the topic begins: The hero crosses watery
wastes impelled by power beyond his will; he arrives on islands or
strands beyond the reach of the real; and there he finds a perfection
of soul that makes actuality, when he returns to it, endurable. This
is the ancient understanding of the travails of Odysseus, and it was not
unknown to the Elizabethans. It seems possible to me that the story
of Odysseus and its moral meaning may have colored for them the
dramatic procedure of *The Tempest.*

   To an Elizabethan who had the Greek and the stomach for the
task, a number of commentaries explained the meaning that Homer
hid beneath the literal fiction of Odysseus' wanderings in the islands.
Armed with the popular notion that noble doctrine should be sugared
with story, the Elizabethan might come to the labor of reading the
Homeric commentaries of Heraclitus, Eustathius, Porphyrius, and the

---

[6] *Ibid.,* V. 19–20. The same tale appears in the pseudo-Aristotle, *De Mirabilibus
Auscultationibus,* in *Opera,* ed. Bekker (Berlin, 1831), II. 836.

pseudo-Plutarch with more interest than these ancient exegetes can beget in us. The *De Vita et Poesi Homeri* of the pseudo-Plutarch argues that the Homeric poems are philosophical accounts of the physical nature of the world as well as ethical expositions of the vices and virtues.[7] Heraclitus demands that both epics be read as allegories. Only the ignorant, says he, who do not understand the language of allegory, who are incapable of recognizing truth, and who reject analogical interpretation, cling to the appearances of fiction. As a consequence, these ignoramuses are deaf to the voice of philosophy; but the wise, who hear the voice, go forward, accepting the *Iliad* and the *Odyssey* as guides to holy truth.[8] Some samples of this truth are apropos.

"All of the wanderings of Odysseus," writes Heraclitus, "if one regards them closely are great allegories. Homer invented this man in order to expound the nature of virtue and to serve the teaching of wisdom, because he detests the manifold vices that consume men." [9] The lotus is, consequently, a symbolic plant; it represents those pleasures and delights that cause men to forget their true home. The fact that Odysseus passes close to slaves of exotic and barbarian pleasures and is not tempted makes a shrewd moral point.[10] His temperance is further illustrated when he refuses, though starving, to eat the cattle of Helios. The temptations of Circe's island are obvious, but the reader must also understand that Hermes, who aids Odysseus in subduing the goddess, is a symbol, not a god in presence. Hermes is reason and dwells in Odysseus. When they seem to be talking, it is Odysseus reflecting or conversing with himself. The magic moly is the sign of reason; hence, it has black roots to represent the hard first steps in knowledge, but it terminates in a bright flower.[11] Such is the pagan reading; now we can continue this knotty explanation of Odysseus' wanderings by turning to Bishop Eustathius for the Christian message.

The island goddess Calypso, says Eustathius, is literally "the fair goddess," but she is also two abstract ideas. She is the body that confines the soul; and Odysseus, aided by Hermes-Reason, gives her up in order to return to Penelope, or Philosophy. There is a second meaning. Calypso is the child (the thought) of Atlas, so she is clearly the science of astronomy and astrology. Odysseus, we know from other places in

[7] Plutarch, *Opera*, ed. Dübner (Paris, 1875), V, 104.
[8] *Quaestiones Homericae*, ed. Oelmann (Leipzig, 1910), p. 4.
[9] *Ibid.*, pp. 91–92.
[10] *Ibid.*, pp. 94–95.
[11] *Ibid.*, pp. 96–97; Alcinous is equated with the Epicurean philosophy; and hence, his kingdom has no charm for the Platonist Odysseus. Cf. pp. 105–6.

the epic, was well versed in starlore; but after Calypso has furthered
his education in this science, he, realizing that it is only a minor branch
of learning, returns to his wife, whose daily weaving and unweaving
of her web shows that she is Philosophy.[12] So Eustathius finds moral
readings here and in other episodes in the epic to support his conviction that the poem is a treatise on the education of men.[13]

There is no question that the sixteenth century saw these moral
meanings in the stormblown ventures not only of Odysseus but also
of his Latin reflection, Aeneas. When Chapman inscribed his translation of the *Odyssey* to the Earl of Somerset, he stated that a moral
reading of the poem was a requirement. The *Iliad*, he writes, begins
with the word "wrath," the *Odyssey* with "man"; the latter poem is,
consequently, superior in moral instruction.

> In one, Predominant Perturbation; in the other, overruling Wisedome;
> in one, the Bodie's fervour and fashion of outward Fortitude to all pos-
> sible height of Heroicall Action; in the other, the Mind's inward, con-
> stant and unconquered Empire, unbroken, unaltered with any most in-
> solent and tyrannous infliction. . . . Nor is this all-comprising Poesie
> phantastique, or meere fictive, but the most material and doctrinall
> illations of Truth, both for all manly information of Manners in the
> yong, all prescription of Justice, and even Christian pietie, in the most
> grave and high-governd. To illustrate both which in both kinds, with all
> height of expression, the Poet creates both a Bodie and a Soule in them—
> wherein, if the Bodie (being the letter, or historie) seemes fictive and
> beyond Possibilitie to bring into Act, the sence then and Allegorie
> (which is the Soule) is to be sought—which intends a more eminent
> expressure of Vertue, for her lovelinesse, and of Vice, for her uglinesse,
> in their severall effects, going beyond the life than any Art within life
> can possibly delineate. Why then is Fiction to this end so hatefull to
> our true Ignorants? [14]

Heraclitus comes to life in the last sentence, but the tone of the whole
passage implies that he was never really dead.

If Odysseus' journeys to the storm-set islands were allegories of the
moral testing and education of men, we can, perhaps, assume that the
voyage of Prospero and that of his enemies might have the same intent.
We must notice at the start that the islands of the Greek epic and that
of *The Tempest* are not exactly alike. The Greek islands are fantastic
garden spots, direct mirrorings of the Isles of the Blest; they are not
unlike the one that Diodorus' sailors found in the broad ocean. The

---

[12] *Commentarii ad Homeri Odysseam* (Leipzig, 1825), I. 16–17.
[13] *Ibid.*, II. 4–5; Odysseus listens to the sirens because it is good for a philosopher
to hear the poets.
[14] Homer, Chapman transl., ed. Nicoll (New York, 1956), II. 4–5.

Renaissance had not forgotten the Homeric islands, and we have only
to turn to Ronsard's poem on Calypso to recapture their charm.

> Terre grasse et fertille,
> Lieu que les Dieux avoient pour eux esleu,
> Pour tes forests autrefois tu m'as pleu,
> Pour tes jardins, pour tes belles fonteines,
> Et pour tes bords bien esmailles d'areines.[15]

> [Rich and fertile land,
> Place chosen by the gods for their own,
> Once for your forests you did please me
> And for your gardens, for your beautiful fountains,
> For your slopes studded so with glistening brass.]

Prospero's island, like Perdita's Arcadia, suffers intrusions from reality.
In most instances we see the island through the eyes of Caliban, the
only animal survivor now that its Circe (Sycorax) is dead. Through
these banal eyes, we see that the island has fresh springs, brine pits,
barren and fertile places, bogs, fens, flats. We learn through other eyes
that there are desolate spots where there is "neither bush nor shrub."
But it also has grassplots, "lush and lusty"; it produces berries, pignuts,
crabapples, filberts, and limes. It is, however, no thornless Eden, for—
once again Caliban tells us—it has "toothed briars, sharp furzes, pricking goss, and thorns."

When Prospero set foot on the island, it was not unlike Circe's
Aeaea, not honored "with a human shape." The blue-eyed witch
Sycorax (a true half-sister of the daughter of Helios), whose antiquity
is attested by her ability to "control the moon," ruled the island with
"earthy and abhorred commands." The child of this earthy enchantress
is naturally earthy, an animal bent on animal pleasures, filled with
animal desires, haunted by animal fears. Odysseus broke the spell of
Circe; but Prospero, although he can undo the black magic of Sycorax,
is unable to raise Caliban to human estate. The island has also some
colors of Ogygia; but of Calypso, who sang with sweet voice while she
wove on her loom with a golden shuttle, only the music and the
knowledge are left. It is this music that Ferdinand hears—the singing
of the invisible Ariel—before he sees Miranda, and so he speaks as
Odysseus may have spoken when, fresh from Hell and sea-peril, he
saw the humane goddess "who took him in and treated him kindly."

> Most sure, the goddess
> On whom these airs attend. Vouchsafe my prayer

---

[15] *Œuvres*, ed. Vaganay (Paris, 1924), IV. 218.

> May know if you remain upon this island,
> And that you will some good instruction give
> How I may bear me here.[16]

The music that diabolic magic imprisoned in a tree, heavenly magic released, and now it has charms even for beast-hearted men. "The isle is full of noises," says Caliban, "sound, and sweet airs, that give delight and hurt not." [17] The two clowns, made beasts by wine, "lifted up their noses/ As they smelt music."[18] If in these respects the island has recollections of Ogygia, there are reminders of Calypso in both Prospero and Miranda: her wisdom in the father, her beauty in the girl. In Miranda there is a further quality of the Greek woman—the pity that only a goddess can have for men. "For I have a proper mind," says Calypso as she walks to the beach with Odysseus, "and my heart is not iron but as pitiful as yours." [19]

Prospero's island also brings to mind other literary islands of later date. Honorius, who wrote two thousand years after Homer, tells about the Island Perdita, charming, fertile, unknown to men. "Once you have found it by chance, if you leave it, you will never find it again." [20] This island like all lost islands—Atlantis, the island of the sybil who prophesied the birth of Christ, the islands of Delos unknown before the Flood—haunted the imagination of many generations. Sir John Mandeville knew many of these islands, and we can follow his sail from Crues to Lamary to Silha to the Isle of Bragman.[21] But the most popular legend which brought together saints, men of sin, and visions, is the story of Brendan, the Irish Odysseus, who found Island Perdita (lost by Honorius), the Island of Sheep (where the kine of the Sun are remembered), and the "Paradisus Avium" (where a great white tree was filled with Ariels).[22] He who has visited the islands of antiquity and of the Middle Ages has no difficulty in finding his way to those of the Renaissance.

*   *   *

[16] I. ii. 420–25.
[17] III. ii. 144–45.
[18] IV. i. 177–78.
[19] V. 190–91.
[20] *De Imago Mundi* (*PL*, CLXXII. 132–33).
[21] *The Travels,* ed. Pollard (London, 1915), pp. 108–15, 119–39, 192–98.
[22] *The Anglo-Norman Voyage of St. Brendan by Benedeit,* ed. Waters (Oxford, 1928), pp. 23, 28–29; see also *St. Brandan,* ed. Wright (London, 1844); *Sanct Brandan,* ed. Schröder (Erlangen, 1871); *Les voyages merveilleux de Saint Brandan,* ed. Francisque-Michel (Paris, 1878); *Die altfranzosische prosaübersetzung von Brendans Meerfahrt,* ed. Wahlund (Upsala, 1900); *An old Italian version of the Navigatio Sancti Brendani,* ed. Waters (Oxford, 1931).

The masque, it must be noticed, is structurally bound to the play through the character of Iris, who, in her mythological guises, is the messenger of the goddesses, a virgin,[23] and, better still, sister to the Harpies.[24] It is a part that Ariel could and did play with great skill.

The masque is one of the dramatic centers of the play, and in its simple theme of immortality through generation we have again the doctrine that lighted most of Shakespeare's days on earth. Though I shall return to this, I want first—now that the island is for the moment so plainly a place of vision—to ponder the secondary emphasis in this play, as in previous ones, on the world of vision and dream. This emphasis is finely stated when Prospero speaks his famous lines concluding the revels.

> These our actors,
> As I foretold you, were all spirits, and
> Are melted into air, into thin air;
> And like the baseless fabric of this vision,
> The cloud-capped towers, the gorgeous palaces,
> The solemn temples, the great globe itself,
> Yea all which it inherit, shall dissolve,
> And like this insubstantial pageant faded
> Leave not a rack behind. We are such stuff
> As dreams are made on; and our little life
> Is rounded with a sleep.[25]

Within the boundaries of this utterance, Shakespeare accepts the philosophy of mortal existence against which the dark plays protest. Because once again he accepts the promise of the masque, the benediction of Juno and the rewards of Ceres, he can also accept the necessary condition that men and their works, as he knew them, are only visions and will dissolve like summer clouds. If the world that each man has made is a vision, then life as each man possesses it is a dream. To expound this idea, sturdy tradition aids us mortals, who like Christopher Sly have only "an after-dinner's sleep" between youth and age, to comprehend the topics that Prospero's aria reveals.

First, it is interesting to scrutinize the dream metaphors in *The Tempest*. Miranda, mindful of her childhood, says that it was "rather like a dream than an assurance"; and Ferdinand, under the spell of both the girl and her father, finds his "spirits" all bound up "as in a dream." The Boatswain, no philosopher, thinks of dreams when he searches his mind for a figure to express the rapid course of time: "On

[23] Theocritus, *Eidyllion* XVII. 134; Vergil, *Aeneid* V. 610.
[24] Hesiod, *op. cit.*, 266, 780.
[25] IV. i. 146–57.

a trice, so please you,/ Even in a dream, were we divided from them."
Even Caliban, earth and filth that he is, brings dream and music together to describe the island:

> and then, in dreaming,
> The clouds methought would open, and show riches
> Ready to drop upon me, that when I waked
> I cried to dream again.[26]

Throughout Shakespeare's plays—and the custom is not peculiar to
him alone—*dream* is a metaphor of *life*, as if it were difficult to separate the life of dreams from conscious existence.

The origin of this imagistic comparison begins, I suppose, with
human time. The Gentile hero, Job, whose poet almost got him
canonized, says of the lot of man: "He shall fly away as a dream, and
shall not be found: yea, he shall be chased away as a vision of
night." [27] Across the lines of Jehovah's territory were less consecrated
poets who would agree. For Pindar, "man is a shadow's dream." [28]
and Sophocles describes men in the *Ajax* as "dreams or shadows." [29]
Aristophanes summons men, who "pass like dreams of sorrow," to
listen to the singing of the *Birds*.[30] The Middle Ages improved on these
images of the Greeks and the Romans to such an extent that its child
and reformer, the optimistic Petrarch, could complain about the
dreamlike quality of existence. He writes to Giacomo Colonna that
life is a dream or shifting fancy. "Illa relegenti, totam mihi vitam
meam, nihil videri aliud quam leve somnium, fugacissimumque
phantasma." [31] It is interesting that this passage comes from a letter
on the subject of the vanished glories of Rome, a city that had long
been the subject of meditations on the transitoriness of mortal achievement.

Prospero's reverie about "cloud-capped towers," "gorgeous palaces,"
and "solemn temples" is a metropolitan intrusion into the primitive
island realm. The former duke remembers the land across the waters,
the cities of Carthage or of the Italian mainland. "The great globe itself" may be a playful allusion to the theater on the Bankside, and
the whole speech may wave away the theatrical world of painted cloth
and tinsel; but this is not a speech to father laughter or even smiles,

[26] III. ii. 149–52.
[27] Job 20:8.
[28] *Pyth.* 8. 95–96.
[29] 126.
[30] 686–87.
[31] *Opera* (Basel, 1554), p. 667. ["Upon reflection it seems to me that my entire
life is nothing more than a vague dream, a shifting illusion."]

for its conclusion is grave and its total import is serious. Man passes and so does what he makes. "My weakness . . . my old brain . . . my infirmity . . . my beating mind." The mind of the Renaissance reader is directed by Prospero's words not to the island or to England, but to Rome, the ruined imperial city, where man had pondered for many generations on the impermanence of life and art.[32]

[32] There was present in the imperial Romans, who looked on the ruins of Athens ("vacuae Athenae," says Horace in *Epistulae* II. 2. 81), a modest sense of personal unworthiness and the melting glory of man; nonetheless, they were equally possessed by a reassurance that man's material remainders contain and preserve him. An anonymous late Latin poet might write a poignant epitaph of the great city in which the autumnal music of the Middle Ages is audible (*Anthologia Latina*, ed. Riese [Leipzig, 1922], I. 267), yet the view of the mighty city stirred emotions far more deep.

The Tempest

by A. D. Nuttall

For the nineteenth-century critics of our first chapter,* proving *The Tempest* an allegory and proving it metaphysical were very nearly the same thing. It might be objected that if only we would revive the much-despised opposition between allegory and metaphysics we might be lifted out of this confusing state of affairs; either a poem is allegorical—that is, a fictitious reification of qualities, etc.—or else it is metaphysical, in which case the reification, since it is ontologically asserted, must be taken as literal; hence a poem must be described as either metaphysical or allegorical, certainly not both. Unfortunately, this lucid distinction proves to be of little use when applied to actual specimens of metaphysical/allegorical poetry, since, when the metaphysician wishes to make an ontological assertion, he is seldom *able* to make it literally at all. It is evident that almost all those who have wished to call *The Tempest* allegorical have done so on the ground that it represents metaphysical truths about the world allegorically.

That Shakespeare's poetry betrays a tendency towards metaphysics is, I think, impossible to deny. The suggestion that his metaphysical imagery may be solely intensive in function we have already considered and rejected.[1]

Allegoristic criticism was almost normal in the nineteenth century.

From "The Tempest" by A. D. Nuttall. From Two Concepts of Allegory *(New York: Barnes & Noble, Inc.; London: Routledge & Kegan Paul, Ltd., 1957), pp. 154–60. Copyright © 1967 by A. D. Nuttall. Reprinted by permission of the publishers.*

* [The author has traced the course of romantic criticism of *The Tempest* through the German Schlegel and Heine, the English Mrs. Jameson, Edward R. Russell and J. W. Mackail, the French Victor Hugo and the American James Russell Lowell.]

[1] See above, pp. 123–25. [In *Two Concepts of Allegory:* "If Dante describes Beatrice as heavenly, we are inclined to believe that he means what he says. But if a twentieth century débutante uses the same word to describe her fiancé, we accept it as a mere intensive . . . The question is, then, which does Shakespeare resemble more closely, Dante or the débutante?"]

79

In the twentieth, though still vigorous,[2] it has come to be considered eccentric. But one good result of the general retreat from enthusiastic allegorizing is that when a critic does brave disapproval, and allegorize, we can be tolerably sure that he is describing the play, and not just indulging in verbal high flights of his own.

The twentieth-century arguments for describing *The Tempest* as a metaphysical allegory may be classified under two heads; first those drawn from a comparison of the story-patterns of the late Romances with one other and with the plots and imagery of the earlier Tragedies; second, arguments drawn from the internal character of *The Tempest* itself, its characterization, treatment of morality, use of the supernatural. The first class may be represented by G. Wilson Knight[**] and E. M. W. Tillyard and the second by Derek Traversi and Patrick Cruttwell.

The former critics point out that the late Romances, *Pericles, Cymbeline, The Winter's Tale,* and *The Tempest,* are all concerned with restoration and reconciliation of persons thought to be dead. The recurring feature of the storm is associated with their loss, and music with their reconciliation. This pattern may be compared with another pattern, discernible in the tragedies, in which the breakdown and death of a man is externally reflected in violent storm, and a hint of reconciliation beyond the grave is held out in the metaphors used by the heroes in their "moments of fifth act transcendental speculation." [3] It is thus argued that the Romances in their veritable reconciliation after tempests represent an acting out of those metaphors. It is therefore suggested that they are symbolic of a theological after-life in which all manner of things shall be well. The necessity of supposing that Shakespeare intends a life beyond the grave may well be questioned, particularly since the most explicit metaphysics in *The Tempest* is to be found in the speech in which Prospero stresses the transitoriness of this life which is rounded with a sleep (IV. i. 146–63). So long as eternal happiness is conceived in terms of extended duration, it will be difficult to find unequivocal Shakespearian support for it.

But the relation of the story-pattern of the Romances to that of the Tragedies could be accounted for with a more modest set of presumptions. For example, one might suggest that Shakespeare thought what a wonderful wish-fulfilment type of play could be written if one gave these tragic heroes their whole desire, in this world; if, after all, the beloved person were shown never to have died at all.

---

    [2] The most elaborate of all *Tempest* allegorizings was published in 1921—Colin Still's *Shakespeare's Mystery Play, a study of "The Tempest."*
    [**] [See above, pp. 20–24.]
    [3] G. W. Knight, *The Crown of Life,* London 1948, p. 208.

The dramatic use of the delightfulness of reconciliation after all hope has been lost does not necessarily imply a theological belief in resurrection. If *The Tempest* is really to be taken as an account of survival after death, since it certainly is not literal it must undoubtedly be allegorical. However, I should be much happier with the alternative suggestion, hazier and perhaps unpalatable to Christian sensibilities, that the "story" of life after death and the story of *The Tempest* both stand as myths of some mysterious state of affairs, closely connected with moral questions, which may elude literal description together.

This approach is extremely unmanageable and vague, and perhaps it is for that very reason that it admits more readily an alliance with the second approach, the approach by way of the nature of characterization and treatment of ethics in the last plays. There are indeed certain features in the Romances which are easily connected with the separation and "eternizing" of love-value which we found in the Sonnets and elsewhere.[4] D. A. Traversi says, of Florizel's comparison[5] of Perdita to wave of the sea in *The Winter's Tale* (IV. iii. 140 ff.):

> This image, like the speech of which it forms a part, is, of course, much more than a beautiful piece of decorative poetry. It is rather the particular expression of a vital theme of the play . . . the relation between the values of human life which postulate timelessness, and the impersonal "devouring" action of time which wears these values ceaselessly away. The wave image conveys perfectly the necessary relation between the mutability of life and the infinite value of human experience which it conditions, but which is finally incommensurate with it.[6]

Traversi is quick, too, to point out the association in *The Tempest* of supernatural imagery with intuitions of value.[7] Yet the task is less easily performed for *The Tempest* than it is for *The Winter's Tale*. What we may call the Affirmation of Paradise has in *The Tempest* a far less confident tone. Miranda's first perception of the "noble vessel" has a visionary quality, yet it is belied, as Traversi acknowledges, by the presence of the plotters in the ship. In *The Tempest* alone of the Romances the divine masque is broken up in confusion. The whole play, as compared with *The Winter's Tale*, is strangely perverse, like a piece of flawed glass. Bonamy Dobrée, in a brilliant essay,[8] pointed out the unique flavour of *The Tempest*, more shimmering, less full-bloodedly confident in its paradisal intuitions than its immediate

---

[4] See above, esp. pp. 123–28 [In *Two Concepts*].
[5] Quoted above, p. 44 [In *Two Concepts*].
[6] *Shakespeare: The Last Phase*, London 1954, pp. 151–52.
[7] *Ibid.*, e.g. pp. 202, 207.
[8] "The Tempest," *E & S*, NS V (1952), pp. 13–25. [See above, pp. 47–59.]

predecessors; the wooing of Ferdinand, though piercingly ideal, is
less warm than the wooing of Florizel; the forgiveness of Prospero has
a touch of the priggish Senecan.

It is as if a second wave of scepticism has passed over the poet. It is
quite different from the coprologous indignation of *Troilus and
Cressida*. He no longer, for the sake of one transgression, denies the
authenticity of love itself. But a reservation as to the truth-value of
the assertions love provokes seems to have reappeared. Time, the old
grey destroyer of the Sonnets, was not, after all, put down by love.
After the enthusiastic reaffirmation of the later Sonnets and the first
three Romances, a sadder and more complex reaction has set in,
slightly ironical perhaps, but not at all cynical. The world has not been
wholly redeemed by love; look at it. The subjective vision of the lover
may transcend objective facts, but it does not obliterate them. The
lover has one level, the hater another; perhaps there are a thousand
more such levels, each as unreal as the rest.

Thus the quasi-mystical ethical intuitions are undermined by a
doubt about reality, about the comparative status of different kinds of
perception. My summary of the play in the first half of this chapter
was, of course, selective. It may be as well to proclaim here the principle of selection involved. I was concerned to show Shakespeare's
preoccupation, throughout the play, with the more nearly subliminal
aspects of perception. It is as if Shakespeare himself became concerned,
as I was in the third and fourth chapters of this book, to retreat into
the preconceptual area of the mind. The chapters and the play have,
in a sense, very similar subject-matter. Certainly, *The Tempest* is not
related to that psychological theorizing in just the same way as the
poetic specimens I cited were related to it. Those poems *exemplified*
the indeterminate, configurative imagination. *The Tempest* is, for
much of its length, *about* people configurating, imagining without
actualizing, and so on. Patrick Cruttwell argues[9] that Shakespeare in
his last plays began to take seriously the allegorical/transcendental
images of his youthful poetry. In *The Winter's Tale*, indeed, it may
be that an ontological force is given to such imagery. But in *The
Tempest* the prominence given to the ambiguous lower reaches of our
conceptual and perceptual apparatus infects all ontological dogmatism
with uncertainty. Shakespeare repeatedly restricts his characters to the
primitive stage of perception in their apprehension of the island and
its denizens. In this way he builds up a sense of a shimmering multi-
plicity of levels, which, together with the gratuitous operations of the
supernatural, produce in the audience a state of primitive apprehen-

---

[9] *The Shakespearean Moment*, London 1954, pp. 73–106.

sion similar to that in which the characters find themselves. We are given the impression that the island may, after all, belong wholly to the unassertive world of dreams and ambiguous perceptions. Such material is naturally baffling to the critic who wishes to sort out symbol and statement. The allegorical exegete feels he has been cheated of his proper prey.

But we have also to reckon with the intuitions of value which are expressed in the meeting of Ferdinand and Miranda, and also (possibly) in the masque. That value is in these passages supernaturally conceived according to the logic treated in the earlier chapters of this book, I have little doubt. But it is somewhat puzzling to encounter these intuitions in a context so instinct with the atmosphere of ambiguous imagery. The proper relation of these ethical intuitions to the more elusive intuition that the island is only a dream or figment of the configurative imagination is difficult to determine. Certainly there is no sign of any attempt on Shakespeare's part to postulate a *genetic* relationship, to suggest that primitive configurations are the psychological parents of intuitions of value. After all, the two elements are presented in a totally different manner, the first involving the use of metaphor, the second dramatically. The imaginary status of the island is hinted by the behaviour of the characters, sometimes baffled, sometimes inconsistent. The value-intuitions are explicitly stated, by certain characters in theological imagery, and also (possibly) in the terms of a mythological spectacle. Yet it is easy to feel that some part of the vague scepticism created by the recurrence of half-subliminal perceptions has attached itself to the lovers and the persons of the masque. The differing visions which the castaways have of the island[10] may be held to throw a pale cast of doubt on the vision of Ferdinand when he falls in love with Miranda. We must allow that Shakespeare's motive in associating perceptual ambiguity with supernatural encounters is quite different from the motive behind chapter III*** of this book. He is not concerned to provide an instantial correlative for universals. But in our inquiry into perceptual imagery we discovered the peculiar indulgence of that area of the mind to the combining of things incompatible and the admission of things impossible. It is surely this character which it is Shakespeare's object to exploit. That property of the imagination which makes possible the instantial "universal" is the same property as that which gives *The Tempest* its peculiar atmosphere of ontological suspension. This Shakespeare effects by giving the imagina-

---

[10] II. i. 46–55.
*** [Nuttall's third chapter tries to find "a psychological basis for the mysterious thing—quality (the 'instantially viewed universal')."]

tive "limbo of possibles" a dramatic impulse in the direction of reality, that is, by backing up the glimpses enjoyed by his characters with just enough magical apparatus to determine us in favour of a supernatural explanation without losing our sense of the "internal" flavour of the experience. The truth is that these ambiguities have at least two functions. If they make the reports of the characters dubious, they make the playwright convincing. We cannot trust characters who contradict one another and continually stumble in their encounters with the supernatural. But we must trust the playwright who shows us both their insights and their stumblings.

Shakespeare has, in a perfectly legitimate manner, contrived to have his cake and eat it. He gives us the heart-tearing intuitions of heavenly value, but in a radically empirical and undogmatic way which disarms the cynical critic. He seems to say, "I have seen this, and this, and this. You receive it as I found it. The interpretation I leave to you." Certainly, the challenge has been accepted!

Is *The Tempest* allegorical? If I have done my work properly, the question should have shrunk in importance. The principal object of this book has been to show that allegorical poetry is more curiously and intimately related to life than was allowed by the petrifying formula of C. S. Lewis. One result of this is that the question "Is this work allegorical?" ceases to have the clear significance it would have for a man to whom allegory, as the most ostentatiously fictitious of all literary forms, is directly opposed to a serious preoccupation with the real universe. Nevertheless, I am willing to give a few arbitrary rulings. The simplified characters of the play are not *ipso facto* allegorical, but it is no great sin to take them as types. The sense that beauty and goodness and harmony are ontologically prior to their subjects does not become full-bloodedly allegorical until the masque, where the spirits, nymphs, etc., may without straining be taken as a mythological acting out of the mystery of the betrothal. It is hardly worth while to call the island itself allegorical ("the mind of man" and so on). Certainly it shimmers between subjectivity and objectivity, presents itself differently to different eyes, yet it will not keep still long enough for one to affix an allegorical label. For the island, as for most of the elements of the play, I should prefer to coin a rather ugly term— "pre-allegorical." Ariel and Caliban of all the characters in the play come nearest to being allegories of the psychic processes, but it would certainly be a mistake not to realize that they are very much more besides. If the suggestion of the unique authority of love and value were only a little more explicit, we might allow the word "allegorical" for the play as a whole, and consider the restoration of the supposedly dead as a myth of this ethic, but, as things are, we cannot.

The minutely perceptive scepticism of *The Tempest* defeats the stony allegorist and the rigid cynic equally. The mystery is never allowed to harden into an ontological dogma to be reduced to symbols or rejected with contempt. Instead we have an extraordinarily delicate and dramatic play, which, until the Last Day makes all things clear, will never be anything but immensely suggestive.

One important claim can be made. The suggestiveness of *The Tempest* is metaphysical in tendency, and the indeterminate *concepts* adumbrated do have the logical oddity which we have followed through from the first chapter. Love *is* conceived as a supernatural force, and any number of protestations of metaphor and apologetic inverted commas cannot do away with the fact that a sort of deification, and therefore *a fortiori* reification has taken place. Whether these concepts should be allowed to be meaningful, or whether they should be permitted only a "merely aesthetic" force (and that presumably spurious) I do not know. The unassertive candour of Shakespeare's imagination has left the question open. But the nineteenth-century allegorists were at any rate concerning themselves with the right (i.e., the peculiar) sort of concept. Their heresy is less than that of the hard-headed, poetry-has-nothing-to-do-with-ideas school. Their claims to have found *the* exclusive allegorical interpretation may be left to their foolish internecine strife, but their noses told them truly that the smell of metaphysics was in the air. If we look upon their effusions less as appraisals of the play than as reactions to it, they will be more acceptable. We may think of them as we think of the women who miscarried on seeing the Eumenides of Aeschylus: as critics they may have been injudicious, but as an audience they were magnificent—though perhaps a little too lively.

PART TWO

View Points

A. C. Bradley

In later days, in the drama that was probably Shakespeare's last complete work, the *Tempest,* this notion of the transitoriness of things appears, side by side with the simpler feeling that man's life is an illusion or dream, in some of the most famous lines he ever wrote:

> Our revels now are ended. These our actors,
> As I foretold you, were all spirits and
> Are melted into air, into thin air:
> And, like the baseless fabric of this vision,
> The cloud-capp'd towers, the gorgeous palaces,
> The solemn temples, the great globe itself,
> Yea, all which it inherit, shall dissolve
> And, like this insubstantial pageant faded,
> Leave not a rack behind. We are such stuff
> As dreams are made on, and our little life
> Is rounded with a sleep.

These lines, detached from their context, are familiar to everyone; but, in the *Tempest,* they are dramatic as well as poetical. The sudden emergence of the thought expressed in them has a specific and most significant cause; and as I have not seen it remarked I will point it out.

Prospero, by means of his spirits, has been exhibiting to Ferdinand and Miranda a masque in which goddesses appear, and which is so majestic and harmonious that to the young man, standing beside such a father and such a wife, the place seems Paradise,—as perhaps the world once seemed to Shakespeare. Then, at the bidding of Iris, there begins a dance of Nymphs with Reapers, sunburnt, weary of their August labour, but now in their holiday garb. But, as this is nearing its end, Prospero "starts suddenly, and speaks"; and the visions vanish. And what he "speaks" is shown in these lines, which introduce the famous passage just quoted:

From "Lecture VIII, King Lear" by A. C. Bradley. From Shakespearean Tragedy *(London: Macmillan & Co. Ltd., 1905). pp. 328–30.*

Pros. [*Aside*] I had forgot that foul conspiracy
Of the beast Caliban and his confederates
Against my life: the minute of their plot
Is almost come. [*To the Spirits.*] Well done! avoid; no more.
Fer. This is strange; your father's in some passion
That works him strongly.
Mir.   Never till this day
Saw I him touch'd with anger so distemper'd.
Pros. You do look, my son, in a moved sort,
As if you were dismay'd: be cheerful, sir.
Our revels. . . .

And then, after the famous lines, follow these:

Sir, I am vex'd:
Bear with my weakness; my old brain is troubled;
Be not disturb'd with my infirmity;
If you be pleased, retire into my cell
And there repose: a turn or two I'll walk,
To still my beating mind.

We seem to see here the whole mind of Shakespeare in his last years. That which provokes in Prospero first a "passion" of anger, and, a moment later, that melancholy and mystical thought that the great world must perish utterly and that man is but a dream, is the sudden recollection of gross and apparently incurable evil in the "monster" whom he had tried in vain to raise and soften, and in the monster's human confederates. It is this, which is but the repetition of his earlier experience of treachery and ingratitude, that troubles his old brain, makes his mind "beat," [1] and forces on him the sense of unreality and evanescence in the world and the life that are haunted by such evil. Nor, though Prospero can spare and forgive, is there any sign to the end that he believes the evil curable either in the monster, the "born devil," or in the more monstrous villains, the "worse than devils," whom he so sternly dismisses. But he has learned patience, has come to regard his anger and loathing as a weakness or infirmity, and would not have it disturb the young and innocent. And so, in the days of *King Lear,* it was chiefly the power of "monstrous" and apparently cureless evil in the "great world" that filled Shakespeare's soul with

[1] Cf. *Hamlet,* III. i. 181:

This something-settled matter in his heart,
Whereon his brains still beating puts him thus
From fashion of himself.

horror, and perhaps forced him sometimes to yield to the infirmity of misanthropy and despair, to cry "No, no, no life," and to take refuge in the thought that this fitful fever is a dream that must soon fade into a dreamless sleep; until, to free himself from the perilous stuff that weighed upon his heart he summoned to his aid his "so potent art," and wrought this stuff into the stormy music of his greatest poem, which seems to cry,

> You heavens, give me that patience, patience I need,

and, like the *Tempest,* seems to preach to us from end to end. "Thou must be patient," "Bear free and patient thoughts."

Lytton Strachey

It is difficult to resist the conclusion that he [Shakespeare] was getting bored himself. Bored with people, bored with real life, bored with drama, bored, in fact, with everything except poetry and poetical dreams. He is no longer interested, one often feels, in what happens, or who says what, so long as he can find place for a faultless lyric, or a new, unimagined rhythmical effect, or a grand and mystic speech. In this mood he must have written his share in *The Two Noble Kinsmen,* leaving the plot and characters to Fletcher to deal with as he pleased, and reserving to himself only the opportunities for pompous verse. In this mood he must have broken off half-way through the tedious history of *Henry VIII;* and in this mood he must have completed, with all the resources of his rhetoric, the miserable archaic fragment of *Pericles.*

Is it not thus, then, that we should imagine him in the last years of his life? Half enchanted by visions of beauty and loveliness, and half bored to death; on the one side inspired by a soaring fancy to the singing of ethereal songs, and on the other urged by a general disgust to burst occasionally through his torpor into bitter and violent speech? If we are to learn anything of his mind from his last works, it is surely this.

And such is the conclusion which is particularly forced upon us by

From *"Shakespeare's Final Period"* by *Lytton Strachey. From* Books and Characters *by Lytton Strachey (London: Chatto & Windus, Ltd., New York: Harcourt, Brace & World, Inc., 1922), pp. 60–64. Copyright © 1922 by Harcourt, Brace & World, Inc.; renewed 1950 by James Strachey. Reprinted by permission of the publishers and Mrs. A. S. Strachey.*

a consideration of the play which is in many ways most typical of Shakespeare's later work, and the one which critics most consistently point to as containing the very essence of his final benignity—*The Tempest.* There can be no doubt that the peculiar characteristics which distinguish *Cymbeline* and *The Winter's Tale* from the dramas of Shakespeare's prime, are present here in a still greater degree. In *The Tempest,* unreality has reached its apotheosis. Two of the principal characters are frankly not human beings at all; and the whole action passes, through a series of impossible occurrences, in a place which can only by courtesy be said to exist. The Enchanted Island, indeed, peopled, for a timeless moment, by this strange fantastic medley of persons and of things, has been cut adrift for ever from common sense, and floats, buoyed up by a sea, not of waters, but of poetry. Never did Sheakspeare's magnificence of diction reach more marvellous heights than in some of the speeches of Prospero, or his lyric art a purer beauty than in the songs of Ariel; nor is it only in these ethereal regions that the triumph of his language asserts itself. It finds as splendid a vent in the curses of Caliban:

> All the infection that the sun sucks up
> From bogs, fens, flats, on Prosper fall, and make him
> By inch-meal a disease!

and in the similes of Trinculo:

> Yond' same black cloud, yond' huge one, looks like a foul bombard that would shed his liquor.

The *dénouement* itself, brought about by a preposterous piece of machinery, and lost in a whirl of rhetoric, is hardly more than a peg for fine writing.

> O, it is monstrous, monstrous!
> Methought the billows spoke and told me of it;
> The winds did sing it to me; and the thunder,
> That deep and dreadful organ-pipe, pronounced
> The name of Prosper; it did bass my trespass.
> Therefore my son i' th' ooze is bedded, and
> I'll seek him deeper than e'er plummet sounded,
> And with him there lie mudded.

And this gorgeous phantasm of a repentance from the mouth of the pale phantom Alonzo is a fitting climax to the whole fantastic play.

A comparision naturally suggests itself, between what was perhaps the last of Shakespeare's completed works, and that early drama which first gave undoubted proof that his imagination had taken wings. The points of resemblance between *The Tempest* and *A Midsummer Night's Dream,* their common atmosphere of romance and magic, the beautiful absurdities of their intrigues, their studied contrasts of the grotesque with the delicate, the ethereal with the earthy, the charm of their lyrics, the *verve* of their vulgar comedy—these, of course, are obvious enough; but it is the points of difference which really make the comparison striking. One thing, at any rate, is certain about the wood near Athens—it is full of life. The persons that haunt it—though most of them are hardly more than children, and some of them are fairies, and all of them are too agreeable to be true—are nevertheless substantial creatures, whose loves and jokes and quarrels receive our thorough sympathy; and the air they breathe —the lords and the ladies, no less than the mechanics and the elves —is instinct with an exquisite good-humor, which makes us as happy as the night is long. To turn from Theseus and Titania and Bottom to the Enchanted Island, is to step out of a country lane into a conservatory. The roses and the dandelions have vanished before preposterous cactuses, and fascinating orchids too delicate for the open air; and, in the artificial atmosphere, the gaiety of youth has been replaced by the disillusionment of middle age. Prospero is the central figure of *The Tempest;* and it has often been wildly asserted that he is a portrait of the author—an embodiment of that spirit of wise benevolence which is supposed to have thrown a halo over Shakespeare's later life. But, on closer inspection, the portrait seems to be as imaginary as the original. To an irreverent eye, the ex-Duke of Milan would perhaps appear as an unpleasantly crusty personage, in whom a twelve years' monopoly of the conversation had developed an inordinate propensity for talking. These may have been the sentiments of Ariel, safe at the Bermoothes; but to state them is to risk at least ten years in the knotty entrails of an oak, and it is sufficient to point out, that if Prospero is wise, he is also self-opinionated and sour, that his gravity is often another name for pedantic severity, and that there is no character in the play to whom, during some part of it, he is not studiously disagreeable. But his Milanese countrymen are not even disagreeable; they are simply dull. "This is the silliest stuff that e'er I heard," remarked Hippolyta of Bottom's amateur theatricals; and one is tempted to wonder what she would have said to the dreary puns and interminable conspiracies of Alonzo, and Gonzalo, and Sebastian, and Antonio, and Adrian, and Francisco, and other shipwrecked noblemen. At all events, there can be little doubt that they would not have had the entrée at Athens.

The depth of the gulf between the two plays is, however, best measured by a comparison of Caliban and his masters with Bottom and his companions. The guileless group of English mechanics, whose sports are interrupted by the mischief of Puck, offers a strange contrast to the hideous trio of the "jester," the "drunken butler," and the "savage and deformed slave," whose designs are thwarted by the magic of Ariel. Bottom was the first of Shakespeare's master-pieces in characterisation, Caliban was the last: and what a world of bitterness and horror lies between them! The charming coxcomb it is easy to know and love; but the "freckled whelp hag-born" moves us mysteriously to pity and to terror, eluding us for ever in fearful allegories, and strange coils of disgusted laughter and phantas-magorical tears. The physical vigour of the presentment is often so remorseless as to shock us. "I left them," says Ariel, speaking of Caliban and his crew:

> I' the filthy-mantled pool beyond your cell,
> There dancing up to the chins, that the foul lake
> O'erstunk their feet.

But at other times the great half-human shape seems to swell, like the "Pan" of Victor Hugo, into something unimaginably vast.

> You taught me language, and my profit on't
> Is, I know how to curse.

Is this Caliban addressing prospero, or Job addressing God? It may be either; but it is not serene, nor benign, nor pastoral, nor "On the Heights."

Frank Kermode

There are points in the play at which Shakespeare uses Caliban to indicate how much baser the corruption of the civilized can be than the bestiality of the natural, and in these places he is using his natural man as a criterion of civilized corruption, as Montaigne had done. At the end of the play we learn Gonzalo's stature; he is not only the good-natured calm old man of the wreck, the cheerful courtier of the second act, and the pure soul of the third; he pronounces the

From *"A Salvage and Deformed Slave"* by Frank Kermode. From The Arden Edi-tion of the Works of William Shakespeare: The Tempest *edited by Frank Kermode (London: Methuen & Co., Ltd.; Cambridge: Harvard University Press, 1958), pp. xxxviii–xliii. Copyright © 1958 by Methuen & Co., Ltd. Reprinted by permission of the publishers.*

benediction, and we see that he was all the time as right as it was
to be, even when the common sense of the corrupt he was transparently
wrong—wrong about the location of Tunis, wrong about the commonwealth, wrong about the survival of Ferdinand. And we see that Nature
is not, in *The Tempest*, defined with the single-minded clarity of a
philosophic proposition. Shakespeare's treatment of the theme has what
all his mature poetry has, a richly analytical approach to ideas, which
never reaches after a naked opinion of true or false.

The poetic definition of Nature in the play is achieved largely by
a series of antitheses with Caliban constantly recurring as one term.
He represents the natural man. This figure is not, as in pastoral
generally, a virtuous shepherd, but a salvage and deformed slave.

Caliban's name is usually regarded as a development of some form
of the word "Carib," meaning a savage inhabitant of the New World;
"cannibal" derives from this, and "Caliban" is possibly a simple
anagram of that word. But though he is thus connected with the
Indian savage, he is also associated, as were the uncivilized inhabitants
of the Indies, with the wild or salvage man of Europe, formerly the
most familiar image of mankind without the ordination of civility.
The origins of this type are obscure,[1] but the wild man was a
familiar figure in painting, heraldry, pageant, and drama.[2] Several
varieties are distinguished; the kind which survived in the drama
was a satyr-type, like Bremo in the old play *Mucedorus,* which was
revived by Shakespeare's company in 1610. Bremo abducts a virgin;
unchastity was a conventional attribute of salvage men, which Shakespeare skillfully exploits. These creatures were believed to occupy
an "intermediate position in the moral scale, below man, just as the

---

[1] It is discussed by R. Withington, *English Pageantry* (1918), 1. 72 ff, and by
E. Welsford, *The Court Masque* (1927), p. 6. Possibly the practice of abandoning
children in forests had something to do with it; some of the survivors, perhaps
subnormal to begin with, might have led a bestial life in the woods. Linnaeus
classified such survivors as a distinct species, *homo ferus*. Conceivably the "Gorilla"
observed by Hanno the Carthaginian has some part in the tradition.

[2] Pictorially the wodehouse, or wodewose, flourished in the thirteenth and four-
teenth centuries (R. van Marle, *Iconographie de l'Art Profane* (1931), 1. 183–91).
The earliest recorded dramatic specimen is in a Paduan entertainment of 1208—
magnus Ludus de quodam homine salvatico (P. Neri, in *Giornale Storico della
Letteratura Italiano*, 1. ix. 49; cited by L. Edwards, "The Historical and Legendary
Background of the Wodehouse and Peacock Feast Motif in the Walsokne and
Braunche Brasses," *Monumental Brass Society Transactions,* VIII. Pt. vii, 300–311).
Then they occur with great frequency. In England, there is a wild man in the
Christmas entertainment of Edward III in 1347, and they are common in Tudor
entertainments, such as the progresses and receptions of Elizabeth. (See Nichol's
Royal Progresses, passim.)

angels were above him. . . They are the link between. . . the settled and the wild, the moral and the unmoral." [3] The term "salvage," used of Caliban in the Folio "Names of the Actors," has thus a restricted meaning, as it has in Spenser. Caliban is a salvage man, and the West Indians were salvage men of a topical kind; hence the Indian element in this natural man.

The next thing the "Names of the Actors" says about Caliban is that he is deformed. He is what Thersites called Ajax, "a very land-fish, languageless, a monster." [4] There were reports from the Indies of curious specimens, and these reports may have influenced some of the things that are said about Caliban in the play;[5] but his deformity is visualized in terms of Old World monsters. Caliban's birth, as Prospero insists, was inhuman; he was "a born devil," "got by the devil himself upon thy wicked dam." He was the product of sexual union between a witch and an incubus, and this would account for his deformity, whether the devil-lover was Setebos (all pagan gods were classified as devils) or, as W. C. Curry infers, some aquatic demon.[6]

Caliban's mother, though associated with reports of devil-worship and witchcraft in the New World, belongs to the Old. She is a power-ful witch, deliberately endowed with many of the qualities of classical witches,[7] but also possessing a clearly defined place in the contem-porary demonological scheme. She is a practioner of "natural" magic, a goetist who exploited the universal sympathies, but whose power is limited by the fact that she could command, as a rule, only devils and the lowest orders of spirits. Prospero, on the other hand, is a theurgist, whose Art is to achieve supremacy over the natural world by holy magic. The Neo-Platonic mage studies the harmonic relation-

---

[3] L. Edwards, *loc. cit.* This idea persisted into the eighteenth century; Lovejoy quotes a poem which includes the lines, "De l'homme aux animaux rapprochant la distance, Voyez l'Homme des Bois lier leur existence" (*The Great Chain of Being* [1936], p. 236).

[4] *Troilus and Cressida*, III. iii. 265.

[5] The closest resemblance is in a beast reported by dos Sanctos in 1597, which had the "eares of a Dog, armes like a Man without haire, and at the elbows great Finnes like a fish," which the native assistants had believed to be "the sonne of the Devill." (Quoted by J. E. Hankins, "Caliban the Bestial Man," *P.M.L.A.* LXII [1947], 794.)

[6] W. C. Curry, *Shakespeare's Philosophical Patterns* (1936), pp. 148–55.

[7] Some of the classical *loci* are: Virgil, *Eclogue* VIII, Horace, *Epode* V, Lucan, *Pharsalia*, I; Ovid, *Met.* VII. 199–207; Seneca, *Medea*, 755–66. These witches had a share in the development of the witches of Renaissance literature. Lyly's *Endimion* has a witch, Dipsa, who says she can "darken the Sunne by my skil, and remoove the Moone out of her course." This traditional power is mentioned in the Faust books, and by Reginald Scot.

ship of the elementary, celestial, and intellectual worlds,[8] and conceives it

> no way irrational that it should be possible for us to ascend by the same
> degrees through each World to the same very original world itself, the
> Maker of all things, and First Cause, from whence all things are, and
> proceed . . .[9]

His object is to "walk to the skie," as Vaughan put it, before death, by ascending through the created worlds to the condition of the angels. His Art is supernatural; the spirits he commands are the dæmons of Neo-Platonism, the criterion of whose goodness is not the Christian one of adherence to, or defection from, God, but of immateriality or submersion in matter. He deals with spirits high in the scale of goodness, and if lesser spirits ("weak masters") are required, the superior dæmon controls them on his behalf. He is *"divinorum cultor & interpres,* a studious observer and expounder of divine things," and his Art is "the absolute perfection of Natural Philosophy." [10] Natural Philosophy includes the arts of astrology, alchemy, and ceremonial magic, to all of which Prospero alludes.[11]

We shall return to the special powers and the learning of the mage Prospero; the point here is that his Art,[12] being the Art of supernatural virtue which belongs to the redeemed world of civility and learning, is the antithesis of the black magic of Sycorax.[13]

[8] For detailed discussion of these topics, see R. H. West's invaluable *The Invisible World* (1939), the fullest treatment of the supernatural in Elizabethan drama; and Hardin Craig, *The Enchanted Glass* (1936), Cap. I.

[9] Cornelius Agrippa, *Occult Philosophy,* translated by J. F. (1651), I. i.

[10] Agrippa, *op. cit.* III. xl.

[11] *E.g.,* I. ii. 181–84; V. i. 1, and the many allusions to ceremonial magic—book, rod, cloak of invisibility, which are the instruments of the "rougher magic" which the mage at a later stage renounces, as Prospero does before confronting Alonso.

[12] Always spelled with the capital in F. This is a recognized method of indicating that it is a technical usage.

[13] This highly important distinction is lost if Prospero is called a black magician, as he often is. The arguments against this view are conclusive but there is no space for them here; they can be deduced from the works of West and Curry. It has been objected that Shakespeare could not have presented at the Court of James I a play openly alluding to a system of magic to which the King was notoriously opposed. But James was well accustomed to such treatment; he himself was often presented as a beneficent magician, and he took pleasure in Jonson's *Masque of Queens,* a brilliant iceberg whose hidden part is a craggy mass of occult learning. He no more took exception to this than he did to the presentation of pagan gods whom he theoretically regarded as devils, because he understood the equation between a fiction of beneficent magic and the sacred power he himself professed as an actual king.

Caliban's deformity is the result of evil natural magic, and it stands as a natural criterion by which we measure the world of Art, represented by Prospero's divine magic and the supernaturally sanctioned beauty of Miranda and Ferdinand.

The last thing the "Names of the Actors" says about Caliban is that he is a slave. We have seen the readiness with which the white man took charge of the New World; Prospero arrived on his island "to be the lord on 't." If Aristotle was right in arguing that "men . . . who are as much inferior to others as the body is to the soul. . . are slaves by nature, and it is advantageous for them always to be under government," and that "to find our governor we should. . . examine into a man who is most perfectly formed in soul and body. . . for in the depraved and vicious the body seems to rule rather than the soul, on account of their being corrupt and contrary to nature,"[14] then the black and mutilated cannibal must be the natural slave of the European gentleman, and, *a fortiori*, the salvage and deformed Caliban of the learned Prospero.

Caliban is, therefore, accurately described in the Folio "Names of the Actors." His origins and character are natural in the sense that they do not partake of grace, civility, and art; he is ugly in body, associated with an evil natural magic, and unqualified for rule or nurture. He exists at the simplest level of sensual pain and pleasure, fit for lechery because love is beyond his nature, and a natural slave of demons. He hears music with pleasure, as music can appeal to the beast who lacks reason; and indeed he resembles Aristotle's bestial man. He is a measure of the incredible superiority of the world of Art, but also a measure of its corruption. For the courtiers and their servants include the incontinent Stephano and the malicious Antonio. Caliban scorns the infirmity of purpose exhibited by the first, and knows better than Antonio that it is imprudent to resist grace, for which, he says, he will henceforth seek. Unlike the incontinent man, whose appetites subdue his will, and the malicious man, whose will is perverted to evil ends, "the bestial man has no sense of right and wrong, and therefore sees no difference between good and evil. His state is less guilty but more hopeless than those of incontinence and malice, since he cannot be improved."[15] Men can abase their degree below the bestial; and there is possibly a hint, for which there is no support in Aristotle, that the bestial Caliban gains a new spiritual dimension from his glimpse of the "brave spirits." Whether or no this

[14] *Politics*, 1254 a-b.
[15] See the valuable essay of J. E. Hankins, *P.M.L.A.* LXII.

is true, he is an extraordinarily powerful and comprehensive type of
Nature; an inverted pastoral hero, against whom civility and the Art
which improves Nature may be measured.

C. J. Sisson

It may be observed that in 1611, the probable date of *The Tempest,*
both Forman and Savory[1] were in full practice in London, and Jonson's
recent *Alchemist* of 1610 was still occupying the stage and people's
thoughts. If Jonson was careful, and Chapman was careful, both care-
less on occasion and punished for their carelessness, we might be sure
that Shakespeare would avoid all possible offence in his introduction
of magic into these late plays. There is clearly no cause of offence in
dream-visions, oracles, soothsayers, or magic music of the spheres, in
Cymbeline, Pericles, The Winter's Tale, and *Henry VIII.* These are
theatrical commonplaces and have no origin in those dangerous and
current forms of magic of which the law and the Privy Council took
cognizance. But *The Tempest* lives and moves throughout in magic.
Prospero is a magician and a conjurer, with all the implements of the
professional practitioner, a book of secret magic learning, a magic
staff, and a magic robe like that donned by Subtle in his dealings with
his victims. He has spirits at his command, with power over the elements, the wind and the seas. Like Oberon in Greene's *James the
Fourth* he can spell-bind men from moving, a known power of witchcraft. And magic music waits upon him.

The effectiveness of *The Tempest* as a play requires that some
measure of assent should be given by the audience to this portrait of
a magician. Otherwise it is a pure fantasy, on the level of modern
pantomime. Certainly Dryden had no doubts upon the subject when
he came to translate *The Tempest* into the idiom of his own day;

> I must confess 'twas bold, nor would you now
> That liberty to vulgar wits allow,
> Which works by magic supernatural things.
> But Shakespeare's power is sacred as a king's.

───────
From "The Magic of Prospero" by C. J. Sisson. From Shakespeare Survey 11
(Cambridge University Press, 1958), pp. 74–76. Copyright © 1958 by Cambridge
University Press. Reprinted by permission of the publisher.

[1] Simon Forman and Abraham Savory were shady practitioners of medicine, of
magic, and of conjuring who were notorious in Shakespeare's London about 1610.

Those legends from old priesthood were received,
And he then writ, as people then believed.
(Davenant-Dryden, *The Tempest*, Prologue.)

Certainly under Charles II men were not so completely enlightened in comparison with Shakespeare's England. In Charles' General Pardon sorcery was specifically excluded from its benefits. And there is ample further evidence in legal proceedings, as in writings of the time. But Dryden's point is clear enough. The submissive assent of an audience for dramatic effect which was required for Shakespeare's play is no longer available in Dryden's theatre and audience, which were more sceptical about magic.

Given this basis of popular belief for Prospero's powers in *The Tempest*, provided for in the laws of England, and paralleled in the life of the time, it was a matter of importance that Prospero as a magician should be disassociated from the evil manifestations of such powers, the more so as he is a rightful sovereign Duke.

There is a famous passage in *1 Henry IV*, Act III, Scene i, Hotspur's baiting of Owen Glendower's claims to magical powers, following upon his claims to supernatural signs and portents marking him off from other men. King Henry has already acknowledged those very claims, referring to him as "that great magician, damned Glendower," "damned" because of his secret alliance with the powers of evil. There is no doubt concerning Hotspur's real respect for Glendower. Why, then, does he go out of his way to make a mock of Glendower's magical art? The conflict, of course, has dramatic effect, and emerges naturally enough from Hotspur's character. A modern audience rejoices in it. Certainly, some of Glendower's talk to Hotspur may have seemed to be "skimble-skamble stuff," but his main claims had to be taken seriously enough. Conjuration was a felony on the statute-book, and Savory among others was tried for it in Shakespeare's time. Two of Elizabeth's Northern Earls were widely believed to practise these arts, Henry Clifford, Earl of Cumberland, commonly spoken of as the Wizard Earl, and Henry Percy, Earl of Northumberland. In *Henry IV*, Glendower is a rebel against the reigning King. There was surely need on grounds of policy to have doubts cast on his magical powers. It was a dangerous matter to suggest any notion that rebellion against a lawful sovereign, or plots against his person, might have the effectual support of supernatural powers. And certainly there was need to distinguish between a wizard sovereign, Prospero, and "damned Glendower," in the exercise of magical arts.

A full account is given by Prospero himself of the origin and nature of his powers. He neglected his duties as Duke, his study being all in "the liberal arts," "transported and rapt in secret studies." Deposed and exiled, the especial favour and protection of Providence rescued him from a sinking, unseaworthy ship. His studies included astrology, and he recognizes the auspicious star guiding him to the restoration of his dukedom. He controls the elements, he can raise storms at sea, and aerial spirits come at his call. His powers are superior to those of Sycorax, a damned witch guilty of terrible sorceries, and therefore banished from Argier, and even could command Setebos, her god, according to Caliban. Ariel, once under her magic mastery, and bound, for refusal to do evil, to a punishment which her powers could not undo, was freed by Prospero's higher powers. Sycorax deals in evil spells and charms, and her spirits take the ill-omened shape of toads, bats and beetles, as with other witches. The distinction is sharply made between the powers of Sycorax derived from evil communion with the devil, the father of her son Caliban, and the powers of Prospero, derived from deep study of the secrets of nature. This is made plainly evident in the instruments of his power, his mantle, his staff, and his book, in which alone his magic resides. His spirits are good spirits, and Ariel's nature is opposed to evil-doing, whereas Caliban is the poisonous child of a wicked dam. Like the master of Rosalind is *As You Like It* in her light-hearted claims to magic, Prospero is "a magician most profound in his art and yet not damnable." He has no dealings whatever with the powers of evil. His spirits are of the air or of the upper world of the elements, not infernal spirits of the underworld of hell. His magic, in fact, is philosophy, in its higher reaches. It is White Magic both in origin and in purpose and effect.

It is very significant, therefore, that we cannot trace in Prospero's exercise of his magic art any parallel to the powers and feats claimed by the professional magicians in contemporary practice, as far as I have found them recorded. Prospero does not "cast figures," and he does not work with incantations. He does not draw circles or utter spells. He charms Ferdinand from moving by the power of his "stick." This power, even if it belonged to Merlin of old in the *Morte d'Arthur*, finds no place in the practice of Savory or of Forman. Nor does Prospero's power to induce sleep in Miranda which, be it observed, is put in action after he has put on his magic mantle at I, ii, 169 ("Now I arise").

The only obvious approach to the known evil powers of witchcraft is, of course, the raising of a tempest to affect the fate of ships at sea, a more particular form of the association of witches with elemental disturbances such as we see in *Macbeth*. King James had reason to recall the manifestation of this power exercised against him and his bride Anne of Denmark, an incident reflected in *Macbeth* in the Witches' persecution of the *Tiger* and its master. It was perhaps sailing pretty near the wind for Shakespeare to introduce this power, though it was necessary to his plot. But it is Ariel who creates the storm: it is the element of air in turmoil, and not the work of devils. And "There's no harm done" in the wreck, as Prospero assures the pitiful Miranda, and not a soul on the ship suffers from his action. All is done to good and desirable ends.

There is a strong classical element in the dramatic picture of Prospero's magic, which tends to remove it further from that contemporary realism which Shakespeare was desirous to avoid as far as he could without denying to his play the necessary response in his audience. There is, for example, evidence enough of his reading of Ovid's *Metamorphoses* in the reflection, both in general ideas and in verbal borrowings, of Ovid's Medea in Book VII. This is particularly marked in Prospero's "Ye elves of hills" speech in V, i, which owes much to Ovid. The episode of the banquet, again, in III, iii, with its spectacular vanishing, is plainly derived from Virgil, where the Harpies devour the food laid before Aeneas and his company in Book III of the *Aeneid*. In this masque-like device a stage-direction runs "Enter Ariel, like a harpy," and presently Prospero praises Ariel for his performance of "the figure of this harpy."

There are disconcerting phrases, indeed, in Prospero's invocation in V, i, which seem inconsistent with the general picture of his white magic and import an element of what he himself calls "rough magic," the violence and chaos of black art. It is difficult to reconcile ourselves, for example, to his claim to have opened graves and to have resurrected the dead. But the fact is that Shakespeare has been unwary in his borrowing from Ovid, and has read too much of Medea into Prospero's speech. For this was one of Medea's especial powers. Here, indeed, and not for the first time, we may truly say that Shakespeare had too much education, not too little. The invocation, in fact, conflicts with his his conception of Prospero as a white magician.

We may be tempted to read into *The Tempest* a symbolical representation of a world in which God, or Providence, exercises direct rule by constant intervention in the person of Prospero. The island is a restricted area, fitted for such a rule, and it is an island of beauty. It is indeed the Utopia of Gonzalo's imagination and desires, free from the complexities of human society in civilized countries, save that it has a sovereign. But that sovereign, Prospero, if all-powerful and all-knowing, is moved by benevolence in his sovereignty, like the love of God. He is capable of anger, even as the wrath of God may turn to the punishment of evil. Justice lies in his hands alone, the image of divine justice in direct operation, free from all the uncertainties of human justice even in delegation from God to King and from King to magistrates and judges.

Tempting as this may be, we should perhaps be better advised to see *The Tempest* as in some degree a companion-piece to *Measure for Measure* in Shakespeare's notable concern in his later plays with problems of justice. There we see the image of divine justice in the Duke delegating his justice to human instruments, and of the imperfections of that human justice exemplified in Angelo. Here we see perhaps in Prospero the learned and philosophical ruler, working justice, righting wrongs, defeating rebellion, in his own right as the Vicar of God in his own country, a visible Providence—a conception that would be grateful to the learned and philosophical King James the First.

Clifford Leech

The accidents of composition may have played their part in the structural achievement of *The Winter's Tale,* but there can be no doubt that Shakespeare in *The Tempest* aimed from the beginning at a firm articulation. This time the central figure was to be, not the offender who comes to repentance, but the sufferer who is also an incarnate Providence, measuring with care his punishments and mercies. Prospero is the dream-figure of ourselves which we all from time to time imagine, elevated by a special dispensation to a position of full authority over our enemies and even our friends, able with a nod to perplex, to chastise, to pardon. He may remind us of Baron Corvo's strangely elevated hero in *Hadrian VII,* who within a short time from the novel's beginning is seated in the papal chair. There is no need for a theophany in this play, for Prospero has himself the divine capacity: when the figures of Juno and Ceres appear in the masque, they are Prospero's spirits, to be invoked and banished at a word. The play will, like *The Winter's Tale,* show sin and punishment and repentance and pardon, but it is lesser figures who will suffer this chain of experiences: in the centre is the deprived Duke of Milan, who will impose his law and finally resume his princely status. But a difficulty lies in the fact that Prospero is indeed a dream-figure. Once he moves back into the society of men, he re-enters the world of flux. Abandoning the authority of magic, he is subject once again to the dangers that he knew, years before, in his duchy. Moreover, there is no sense of finality in the stories of those he punishes and pardons. Antonio and Sebastian receive their rebuke, for their planning of

From "The Structure of the Last Plays" by Clifford Leech. From Shakespeare Survey 11 (Cambridge University Press, 1958), pp. 25–27. Copyright © 1958 by Cambridge University Press. Reprinted by permission of the publisher.

Alonso's murder, in a mere aside; Caliban will "sue for grace" becaue
Prospero is more imposing in his ducal robes, as well as evidently more
powerful, than the drunken Stephano in his borrowed finery; Miranda's dazzlement at the "brave new world" (which includes Antonio
and Sebastian among its "goodly creatures") suggests the reverse of
finality in her story. Prospero at the play's end, implying Alonso's
responsibility for Trinculo and Stephano, admits his own responsibility
for Caliban:

> Two of these fellows you
> Must know and own; this thing of darkness I
> Acknowledge mine. (V. i. 274–76)

In this there is surely a hint of his power's limits, of his belonging
(despite all the authority of magic in the past, of ducal status in the
future) to Alonso's world. Certainly a suggestion that a process is complete is contained in the assertion that henceforth "Every third
thought shall be my grave." The sense of tiredness that is implied here
is indeed not unlike that that finally oppressed Corvo's Hadrian, who,
however, was allowed assassination when the dream of power faded.
But we cannot feel a sense of true completion in Prospero's story:
what Antonios will intrigue against him yet in Milan, what Calibans
will resist his teaching, remain unidentified yet ever potential. His
books, now drowned, have enabled him to discomfit his enemies within
the play. The future stretches ahead for him as it did for Pericles and
Imogen, with the possibility that the play's pattern of events can recur.

Yet it is obvious that Shakespeare in his planning of this play aimed
at conveying a sense of crisis, of the achievement of a decisive moment
in the lives of Prospero and his subjects. The Unities are preserved,
and the play contains frequent time-references that indicate the total
duration of the action as four hours and the rapid sequence of the
several happenings. Moreover, there is a firm Act-structure, not quite
according to the traditional pattern but fairly close to it. It cannot
exactly preserve the pattern, because on the enchanted island there can
be no serious conflict: nevertheless, Shakespeare has arranged for the
opposition to Prospero to reach its fullest development in Act III, and
for the assertion of his power to be increasingly displayed in the succeeding Acts. The total argument, moreover, is presented in five
separately apprehensible units. The first Act is a long exposition
(more than a quarter of the play), and takes us up to Ferdinand's
meeting with Miranda and his immediate subjection to Prospero.
Within this Act we have Ariel's fit of rebelliousness, and Prospero's
stern handling of this is an image of his handling of the three other
rebellions that will be more fully developed in the play. The two

scenes of the second Act show us the arrival of Alonso and his company, and of Trinculo and Stephano: in each instance there is exhibited matter for correction. Then in Act III the three rebellions are handled in turn: Miranda, defying her father's injunctions, visits Ferdinand and confesses her love; Caliban, with Trinculo and Stephano, plots against Prospero; Alonso and the rest, whose rebellion lies in the past, are driven to desperation by the vision of the banquet and of Ariel as a harpy, and Alonso is ready to kill himself. Two of these rebellions are disposed of in Act IV, as Prospero releases Ferdinand from toil and consents to his betrothal, and then employs Ariel and the dog-spirits to chasten Caliban and his allies. The famous lines on the mutability of man's works and of Nature herself come between these two assertions of Prospero's power: they provide a commentary on it which does indeed foreshadow the play's final suggestion that the crisis is not yet, is not within the play's ambit. The last Act gives us the end of the remaining rebellion, and puts loose ends into place. It is noticeable that Prospero's words on his abandonment of magic —"deeper than did ever plummet sound I'll drown my book"—remind us of Alonso's decision in III, iii to follow his son to death:

> I'll seek him deeper than e'er plummet sounded,
> And with him there lie mudded. (III. iii. 101–2)

The abandonment of magic power is, indeed, a kind of death for Prospero. But this ending is a mere re-entry into the flux: as a Duke of Milan, he will become Fortune's subject again. This is part of the undercurrent of the play, in contrapuntal relationship to the Act-structure and the overt affirmation of Prospero's triumph. This undercurrent moves towards the surface at the play's end, and makes it appropriate that, in the Epilogue, Prospero no longer summons elves and demi-puppets but speaks of prayer that may yet bring mercy and pardon.

John Wain

In *The Tempest,* we come straightaway upon two striking differences from the pattern as it has become familiar to us. The preserving

From "In My End Is My Beginning" by John Wain. From The Living World of Shakespeare: A Playgoer's Guide by John Wain (New York: St. Martin's Press, Inc., 1964), pp. 225–27, 229–30. Reprinted by permission of St. Martin's Press, Inc. and Curtis Brown Ltd.

and creative storm comes at the very beginning instead of at mid-point; and it is caused not by Nature but by Art. Prospero, ousted from his dukedom by his brother Antonio, has been thrown on the mercy of the seas in a leaky hulk with his infant daughter. Miranda is thus, like Marina and Perdita, a child of the sea; and Prospero has undergone his own sea-ordeal before imposing it on the other characters. All this was years ago (sixteen years?), and the intervening time has been filled with study and meditation—a counterpart to the long repentance of Leontes.

But Prospero is not another Leontes. To begin with, he is not repentant. Though his loss of the dukedom is obviously to some extent his own fault—this appears even in his own account of it, to Miranda at the opening of the play—he sees his magical studies primarily as an instrument of power, by which he may win back his position. And during the years on the island he has likewise used his knowledge in the service of power. He has, as we should say, "colonized" it. And here the story links up with the contemporary world, with the strange deliverance of the *Sea-Adventure,* the colony in Virginia, and the argument over Nature and Nurture.

One of the few books we can say with fair certainty that Shakespeare owned (as distinct from the many we know he must have read) is John Florio's translation of Montaigne's *Essays* (1603), for the British Museum has a copy of this book with what looks like Shakespeare's signature in it. There, Shakespeare would have taken particular note of the essay "Of the Caniballes," which argued that these fortunate beings are the unspoilt children of Nature:

> They are even savage, as we call those fruits wilde, which nature of her selfe, and of her ordinarie progress hath produced: whereas indeed, they are those which our selves have altered by our artificiall devices, and diverted from their common order, we should rather terme savage.

And again:

> . . . there is no reason, art should gaine the point of honour of our great and puissant mother Nature. We have so much by our inventions surcharged the beauties and riches of her workes, that we have altogether overchoaked her: yet where ever her puritie shineth, she makes our vaine and frivolous enterprises wonderfully ashamed.

This is a strong point of view; it is exactly in line with Perdita's distrust of the art which shares with great creating nature; and if Shakespeare had intended to agree with it, he would have made Caliban beautiful and innocent, instead of (as the Dramatis Personae firmly calls him) "a savage and deformed Slave." Does Shakespeare, then, clash head-on with Montaigne and those who think like him? No, not head-on. It is not Shakespeare's way to give neatly defined answers that can be taken away and applied independently of the works in which they occur. He will teach general lessons, but he will not give blackboard answers to specific problems.

Caliban is a symbolic figure, coming from the same region of Shakespeare's imagination as the witches in *Macbeth*. His mother was Sycorax, a "foul witch," "who with age and envy Was grown into a hoop." Before Prospero arrived, the island was under the rule, not of beneficent Nature, but of this hag, who imprisoned the delicate Ariel while letting the gross Caliban, her offspring, roam unchecked. Prospero's advent was no doubt unfortunate for Caliban, but it was a blessing for Ariel, who gained from it a measure of freedom, with the promise of complete liberation in the end.

Caliban, whose name is a fairly obvious anagram of "Cannibal," has therefore a complex role in the action. On the one hand, he is an indirect argument for Prospero's Art and against the policy of leaving everything to Nature. On the other hand, he has the pathos of the exploited peoples everywhere, poignantly expressed at the beginning of a three-hundred-year wave of European colonization; even the lowest savage wishes to be left alone rather than "educated" and made to work for someone else, and there is an undeniable justice in his complaint:

> For I am all the subjects that you have,
> Which once was mine own king.

Prospero retorts with the inevitable answer of the colonist: Caliban has gained in knowledge and skill (though we recall that he already knew how to build dams to catch fish, and also to dig pig-nuts from the soil, as if this were the English countryside). Before being employed by Prospero, Caliban had no language:

> thou didst not, savage,
> Know thy own meaning, but wouldst gabble like
> A thing most brutish.

However, this kindness has been rewarded with ingratitude; Caliban, allowed to live in Prospero's cell, has made an attempt to ravish Miranda; when sternly reminded of this, he impenitently says, with a kind of slavering guffaw,

> Oh ho! Oh ho!—would it had been done!
> Thou didst prevent me; I had peopled else
> This isle with Calibans.

Our own age, which is much given to using the horrible word "miscegenation," ought to have no difficulty in understanding this passage. Quite apart from an understandable wish not to have his daughter ravished by anyone, Prospero could hardly maintain his rule over an island whose inhabitants were partly Caliban's and partly his own. Small wonder that Caliban is banished to a cell among the rocks, and put on to heavy labour. . . .

> Sometimes a thousand twangling instruments
> Will hum about mine ears; and sometimes voices,
> That, if I then had wak'd after long sleep,
> Will make me sleep again: and then, in dreaming,
> The clouds methought would open and show riches
> Ready to drop upon me; that, when I wak'd
> I cried to dream again.

A character who can talk in this strain is not wholly unsympathetic, however little we should like to meet him on a dark night. "A born devil," Prospero calls on, "on whose nature Nurture will never stick," but the Nature that rules Caliban's being, and will brook no intervention from Nurture, is still a divinity even though cruel.

In a less extreme way, the milder virtues of the pastoral world also get their due in this play. Miranda is the product of Nurture, since she not only comes of noble blood ("a gentler scion") but has been elaborately educated by her father. Nevertheless, she is pastoral in that she has never mixed in corrupting human society, never been subjected to the tawdry city-life that makes vulgarians of such as Trinculo and Stephano. Civilization has its heavy penalties, as no one knows better than the representative of Art, Prospero: when, in rapture, the girl cries out "O brave new world That hath such people in 't," he says drily, " 'Tis new to thee."

In the end, the characters leave the island and go back to civilization, as they always do in Shakespeare; human work has to be carried on, somebody has to govern, the dailiness of life will start up again. The Forest of Arden and Prospero's island, the "wood near Athens" or the Welsh mountains in *Cymbeline*, have one thing in common: they are places where important lessons are to be learnt. Once that is done, the characters go back to their normal business. But it is right that some vision of an ideal simplicity, of a life untrammelled by the hampering demands of law and custom, should persist among them. In *The Tempest*, it is noteworthy that the one character among the shipwrecked party who really enjoys the idea of a golden-age simplicity is Gonzalo, the good old courtier whose generosity to the doomed Prospero parallels that of Antigonus to the infant Perdita, when he fitted his boat out with necessities and even books. As Dr. Johnson pointed out, "being the only good Man that appears with the King, he is the only Man that preserves his cheerfulness in the Wreck, and his Hope on the Island." To the amusement of the two evil sophisticates, Sebastian and Antonio, he seeks to beguile the melancholy of King Alonso, mourning the supposed death of his son Ferdinand, by talking about the ideal commonwealth he would like to set up on such as island as this. His views turn out to be much the same as those of Montaigne—a sure sign that Shakespeare considered those views worthy of a courteous hearing.

> I' the commonwealth I would by contraries
> Execute all things; for no kind of traffic
> Would I admit; no name of magistrate;
> Letters should not be known; riches, poverty,
> And use of service, none; contract, succession
> Bourn, bound of land, tilth, vineyard, none;
> No use of metal, corn or wine, or oil;
> No occupation; all men idle, all;
> And women too, but innocent and pure;
> No sovereignty . . .
> All things in common nature should produce
> Without sweat or endeavour; treason, felony,
> Sword, pike, knife, gun, or need of any engine,
> Would I not have; but nature should bring forth,
> Of its own kind, all foison, all abundance,
> To feed my innocent people.

It may be only a dream, but it is a healing and generous dream, fit to haunt the mind of a just man.

Harry Levin

Such is the argument of Montaigne's whimsical and searching essay, "Of the Cannibals." It poses a reflexive question—who's a barbarian? who's a civilized person? or else, as Melville would ask, who ain't a cannibal?—by drawing a full-length portrait of the noble savage as observed by a family servant who had spent ten years in America. That

From "The Golden Age and the Renaissance" by Harry Levin. From Literary Views *edited by Carroll Camden (Chicago: University of Chicago Press, 1964), pp. 8–10. Copyright © 1964 by William Marsh, Rice University. Reprinted by permission of the publisher.*

happy condition of man, Montaigne is convinced, actually surpasses the fictions about the Golden Age, and a first-hand acquaintance with savages would have jolted the preconceived ideas of such philosophers as Plato. And Montaigne itemizes in his turn:

> It is a nation, would I answer Plato, that hath no kind of traffic, no knowledge of letters, no intelligence of numbers, no name of magistrate nor of public superiority; no use of service, of riches, or of poverty; no contracts, no successions, no partitions, no occupation but idle; no respect of kindred but common; no apparell but natural; no manuring of lands, no use of wine, corn, or metal.

As Montaigne specifies and speculates, he makes it clear in his equilibrating way that he is less concerned with the virtues of savagery than with the vices of self-styled civilization. Hence, after the visiting cannibal has been told about France, he is less impressed with its king than with its extremes of wealth and poverty. The train of speculation ends with a shrug—"But, after all, they wear no trousers"—suggesting, at first glance, that such informants ought not to be taken very seriously. However, Montaigne's expression for trousers is *haut-de-chausses;* the comparative nakedness of the Amerindians is juxtaposed to the ridiculous foppery of the breeches and hose then worn by French courtiers; and the question lingers, who has the last laugh. The ambiguity, as usual with Montaigne, is double-edged.

Montaigne points the way for his avid reader Shakespeare, who was always fascinated by "golden times" and who versified an entire page of the essay as he had read it in the resplendent Elizabethan translation of John Florio. It becomes a speech in the second act of *The Tempest,* a play inspired by the misadventures of certain Anglo-American voyagers; and, like the monologue on order in *Troilus and Cressida* or the tale of the belly and the members in *Coriolanus,* the speech sets forth an ideal from which the dramatic reality deviates. You will remember that Gonzalo, the merry old councillor, makes an attempt to cheer up the shipwrecked King of Naples by playing the childish game of "If I were king." He pretends that the island is his commonwealth, which he would govern by a system contrary to the practices of Europe in all respects, and with such success as to excel the Golden Age.

> All things in common nature should produce
> Without sweat or endeavour. Treason, felony,
> Sword, pike, knife, gun, or need of any engine
> Would I not have; but nature should bring forth,
> Of its own kind, all foison, all abundance,
> To feed my innocent people.

The enumeration of merits evinced and of defects avoided follows
Montaigne specifically: no traffic nor magistrate, no letters nor con-
tracts, no riches nor poverty, no wine, corn, nor metal—in fact, no
sovereignty. The cynical courtiers, Sebastian and Antonio, who keep
interrupting with their banter and who are even then hatching a plot
which completely violates these ideals and subverts Shakespeare's
norms, call attention to the inconsistency here:

> No sovereignty.
>   Yet he would be king on't.

That is the crux of the problem of anarchy: someone must take office.
Responsibility presupposes authority; authority imposes responsibility.
Miranda's "brave new world" turns out, ironically, to be the same old
one.

Prospero, the former Duke of Milan, has preferred his books to the
responsibilities of ruling. Therefore he has been dethroned and exiled
to this enchanted isle; he has gone, perforce, back to nature. His single
slave is Caliban, the animal-like indigene; and though that name is
borrowed, slightly twisted, from Montaigne's essay on the cannibals,
Caliban seems to be a much cruder creature than Montaigne's exem-
plary primitive; for this child of nature is without nurture—education
—and Shakespeare emphasizes the critical difference. Still Caliban can
teach Prospero something about "the qualities of the isle": where the
fresh water or nourishing herbs can be found. His master compounds
that lore with his own book-knowledge to form his fully pondered
art, which has the symbolic guise of natural magic. Thereby he learns
how to become a good ruler and returns to his duchy for the happy
ending. The same lesson of exile and return, of society refreshed by
recourse to the norms of nature, and of art as a mediator between them
shapes the pattern of other Shakespearean plays. One thinks of *The
Winter's Tale,* with its sheep-shearing festival, and above all of *As You
Like It,* where Shakespeare's very title seems to restate Tasso's law, and
the banished Duke in the Forest of Arden with his merry men is reported to "live like the old Robin Hood of England" and to "fleet
the time carelessly as they did in the golden world." Nor is it surprising, when Englishmen pine for the Golden Age, that what should
stand out about it for them is not its gold but its greenery. One could
cite many English witnesses during the sixteenth and seventeenth centuries who, in invoking the Golden Age or more often a golden world,
couple the allure of greenwoods or gardens together with their fears
of enclosure, industry, and urbanization.

Chronology of Important Dates

Shakespeare	The Age

1558
— Accession of Queen Elizabeth.

1564 Birth of Shakespeare.
— Birth of Marlowe.

1572
— Birth of Ben Jonson.

1576
— Construction of The Theater by James Burbage in London.

1582 Marriage to Anne Hathaway.

1583 Birth of Susanna Shakespeare.

1585 Birth of Hamnet and Judith Shakespeare.

1588
— Spanish Armada destroyed.

1592 First reference to Shakespeare as an actor and playwright in Greene's *Groatsworth of Wit*.

1593 *Venus and Adonis* published.
— Theaters closed by the plague

1594 *Lucrece* published.
— (summer 1592 to late spring 1594).

1597 Purchase of New Place, Stratford.

1599–1600 *Julius Caesar, Henry IV, As You Like It, Twelfth Night.*
— Globe Theater built. Essex Rebellion.

1600–1601 *Hamlet.*

1603
— Death of Queen Elizabeth. Accession of King James.

1604–6 *Othello, King Lear, Macbeth.*
— Publication of Part I of Cervantes' *Don Quixote* (1605).

1607–8
— English Separatists (later to found Plymouth Colony in Massachusetts) escape from England to Holland.

109

	Shakespeare	The Age
1608		Acquisition of Blackfriars Theater by Shakespeare's company.
1608–22		Peter Paul Rubens painting in Antwerp. *Raising of the Cross, Descent from the Cross*, etc.
1609–10		Galileo makes the first astronomical telescope and discovers satellites of Jupiter.
1611–12	*The Tempest.* Shakespeare retires to Stratford.	The Authorized (King James) Version of the Bible.
1613		Claudio Monteverdi, first great figure in the history of opera, becomes choirmaster at St. Mark's, Venice.
1616	Death of Shakespeare.	Publication of Part II of Cervantes' *Don Quixote*. Folio edition of Jonson's plays.
1623	First Folio of Shakespeare.	

Notes on the Editor and Contributors

HALLETT SMITH, the editor of this volume, is Professor of English and Chairman of the Division of Humanities and Social Sciences at the California Institute of Technology. He is the author of *Elizabethan Poetry* and has edited Shakespeare's romances and poems for the forthcoming New Riverside edition.

DON CAMERON ALLEN is Sir William Osler Professor of English Literature at the Johns Hopkins University. His published studies in the Renaissance range over many languages and literatures.

A. C. BRADLEY (1851–1935) was the foremost Shakespearian critic of his time. His *Shakespearian Tragedy* is a classic of character interpretation.

BONAMY DOBRÉE is Emeritus Professor of English at the University of Leeds. As an essayist and critic he has published widely and as editor has presided over the Oxford History of English Literature.

NORTHROP FRYE was Principal of Victoria College, the University of Toronto, and is now University Professor there. He is the author of *Anatomy of Criticism*. His Shakespearian studies include *A Natural Perspective* and *Fools of Time*.

FRANK KERMODE is Winterstoke Professor of English at the University of Bristol. He is a magazine editor and critic. His edition of *The Tempest* in the New Arden edition is the best edition of the play. He has edited the tragedies for the forthcoming New Riverside edition.

G. WILSON KNIGHT is Emeritus Professor of English Literature at Leeds University, actor and producer, the author of many books of Shakespeare criticism, including *The Shakespearian Tempest* and *The Crown of Life*.

CLIFFORD LEECH is chairman of the English department at University College, the University of Toronto. He has published books on Shakespeare's tragedies and on Fletcher, Ford, and Webster.

HARRY LEVIN is Irving Babbitt Professor of Comparative Literature at Harvard University. His many volumes of scholarly criticism include one on Marlowe and one on Shakespeare's *Hamlet*.

A. D. NUTTALL is an English philosopher whose study of allegory led him into a consideration of allegorical interpretations of *The Tempest*.

SIR ARTHUR QUILLER-COUCH (1863–1944) was King Edward VII Professor of

English at Cambridge University, a writer of mystery stories and other works, and co-editor, with John Dover Wilson, of *The New Shakespeare*.

CHARLES JASPER SISSON (1885–1966) was Lord Northcliffe Professor of Modern English Literature at the University of London. He edited the complete works of Shakespeare and published a textual study, *New Readings in Shakespeare*.

THEODORE SPENCER (1902–1949) was a poet, critic, and Boylston Professor of Rhetoric at Harvard University. His Lowell lectures of 1942 were published as *Shakespeare and the Nature of Man*.

E. E. STOLL, for many years Professor of English at the University of Minnesota, was the author of such pioneering and influential works as *Art and Artifice in Shakespeare* and *Shakespeare Studies*.

LYTTON STRACHEY (1880–1932) was a popular biographer and essayist, a member of the Bloomsbury group. Though mainly known for his sardonic books on Victorian subjects, he also published *Elizabeth and Essex* and *Books and Characters*.

JOHN WAIN is a novelist, poet, critic, and television producer. His principal Shakespeare criticism is in *The Living World of Shakespeare*.

JOHN DOVER WILSON was best known as the editor of *The New Shakespeare* of the Cambridge University Press. Among his other works are *What Happens in Hamlet*, *The Fortunes of Falstaff*, and *The Essential Shakespeare*.

Selected Bibliography

This brief list should be considered supplementary to the complete volumes from which the selections in this collection have been chosen.

Chambers, E. K., *Shakespearean Gleanings*. London: Oxford University Press, 1944. The chapter on "The Integrity of *The Tempest*" deals authoritatively with the arguments concerning other hands in the play than Shakespeare's.

Curry, W. C., *Shakespeare's Philosophical Patterns*, 2nd ed. Baton Rouge: University of Louisiana Press, 1959. The chapter on "Sacerdotal Science in Shakespeare's *The Tempest*" gives much background on contemporary beliefs about magic.

Doran, Madeleine, *Endeavors of Art: A Study of Form in Elizabethan Drama*. Madison: University of Wisconsin Press, 1954. Excellent historical criticism, illuminating *The Tempest* and other late plays.

James, D. G., *The Dream of Prospero*. Oxford: Clarendon Press, 1967. Recent lectures on *The Tempest* by a stimulating and sensitive critic.

Law, Ernest, *Shakespeare's Tempest as Originally Produced at Court*. Shakespeare Association Pamphlets No. 5, 1920. How the play was produced in the old banqueting hall of Whitehall palace before King James.

Lea, Kathleen M., *Italian Popular Comedy*. Oxford: Clarendon Press, 1934. At II, 443 ff. there is discussion of the relationship between *The Tempest* and Italian *scenari* of the pastoral tradition.

Nosworthy, J. M., "Music and its Function in the Romances of Shakespeare," *Shakespeare Survey* 11 (1958), 60–69. A good account of the music in *The Tempest* and other late plays.

Pettet, E. C., *Shakespeare and the Romance Tradition*. London and New York: Stables Press, 1949. The last chapter, on the romances, provides a useful corrective to Tillyard.

Still, Colin, *The Timeless Theme*. London: I. Nicholson & Watson, 1936, a revision of *Shakespeare's Mystery Play* (London: C. Palmer, 1921). The first and most extreme of the allegorical interpreters of *The Tempest*.

Tillyard, E. M. W., *Shakespeare's Last Plays*. London: Chatto & Windus, 1938. Lectures on the romances from the point of view of the tragic pattern and planes of reality.

Traversi, Derek, *Shakespeare: The Last Phase*. New York: Harcourt, Brace & World, Inc., 1953. Subjective interpretations of the late plays based upon acute close reading.

TWENTIETH CENTURY
INTERPRETATIONS

MAYNARD MACK, *Series Editor*
Yale University

NOW AVAILABLE
Collections of Critical Essays
ON

PAMELA
THE PLAYBOY OF THE WESTERN WORLD
THE PORTRAIT OF A LADY
A PORTRAIT OF THE ARTIST AS A YOUNG MAN
THE RIME OF THE ANCIENT MARINER
SAMSON AGONISTES
THE SCARLET LETTER
SIR GAWAIN AND THE GREEN KNIGHT
THE SOUND AND THE FURY
THE TEMPEST
TOM JONES
TWELFTH NIGHT
UTOPIA
WALDEN
THE WASTE LAND
WUTHERING HEIGHTS

DATE DUE

APR 3 1972	JUN 3 1991	
MAY 4 1972	APR 1 2 1993	
JUL 24 1972	FEB 0 1 1995	
FEB 3	FEB 0 1 1998	
APR 3 73	MAR 1 2 1998	
	FEB 0 9 2005	
FEB 5 1976		
MAR 4 77		
MAR 6 1978		
MAY 7		
MAY 1 9 30		
SEP 2 9 1980		
DEC 2 9 80		
SEP 1		
MAR 7 83		
SEP 2 5 1986		
MAR 3 0 1989		
MAY 2 1 1990		